LANGUAGE AND

Dorothy S. Strickla
Celia Genishi and Donna E

ADVISORY BOARD: Richard Allington, Kathryn Au, Bernice Cullinan, Colette Daiute, Carole Edelsky, Shirley Brice Heath, Connie Juel, Susan Lytle, Timothy Shanahan

(Continued)

For volumes in the NCRLL Collection (edited by JoBeth Allen and Donna E. Alvermann) and the Practitioners Bookshelf Series (edited by Celia Genishi and Donna E. Alvermann), please visit www.tcpress.com.

Bedtime Stories
and Book Reports
Connecting Parent Involvement and Family Literacy

Edited by

Catherine Compton-Lilly
Stuart Greene

Foreword by Patricia A. Edwards
Afterword by Shirley Brice Heath

Teachers College, Columbia University
New York and London

Published by Teachers College Press, 1234 Amsterdam Avenue, New York, NY 10027

Library of Congress Cataloging-in-Publication Data

Bedtime stories and book reports: connecting parent involvement and family literacy / edited by Catherine Compton-Lilly, Stuart Greene; foreword by Patricia Edwards; afterword by Shirley Brice Heath.
    p. cm. — (Language and literacy series)
  Includes bibliographical references and index.
    ISBN 978-0-8077-5135-0 (pbk.) — ISBN 978-0-8077-5136-7 (hardcover)
  1. Education—Parent participation. 2. Home and school. 3. Parent-teacher relationships. I. Compton-Lilly, Catherine. II. Greene, Stuart.
    LB1048.5.B436 2011
    371.19′2—dc22

                                                                                2010017121

ISBN 978-0-8077-5135-0 (paper)
ISBN 978-0-8077-5136-7 (hardcover)

CONTENTS

FOREWORD

The concept of family–school partnerships is relatively simple. It is about a seemingly plausible idea: that teachers should encourage all families to become involved in their children's education and that we should reach out to families in new and different ways. This idea has heavily influenced educational reform over the past decade, and it lies at the center of most school restructuring initiatives. As with most complex reforms, it is difficult to decipher exactly what advocates of school restructuring want by way of family involvement. At some basic level, though, all advocates of restructuring seem to believe that acknowledging that they want families involved in the business of the schools will lead teachers and administrators to restructure how they think about family involvement, which in turn will increase the overall participation of families, and subsequently lead to improved performance of children. Unfortunately, this is not a reality in most schools. I believe like Epstein (1987) that while "parent involvement is on everyone's list of practices to make schools more effective, to help families create more positive learning environments, to reduce the risk of student failure, and to increase student success" (p. 4), this does not automatically occur. Epstein correctly noted that "parent involvement is everybody's job but nobody's job until a structure is put in place to support it" (p. 10). It comes as no surprise that there is little real parent involvement in schools given the lack of support within the infrastructure to foster and support it. Schools seem to assume that merely stating a desire or preference for family involvement is the extent of their responsibility. I believe that there is a historical context for why many of today's schools find themselves in this predicament. My story offers some credence for how parent involvement got sidetracked after the *Brown* decision.

As a child growing up in the Deep South, I remember vividly that the family, the school, and the community contributed to the educational achievement of African American children. I was born and raised in a mid-sized southwestern Georgia community. I entered school a few years after the 1954 U.S. Supreme Court landmark decision *Brown v. Topeka Board of Education,* which declared segregation in education unconstitutional. I grew up in a stable, close-knit neighborhood where I knew many eyes watched me and would tell my Mama when I misbehaved. My elementary school principal and most of my teachers lived in my neighborhood. Consequently, there were many opportunities outside of school for my principal and teachers to talk with my parents about my progress and behavior in school. My principal, teachers, neighbors, as well as my parents all shared and reinforced similar school and family values.

Before school desegregation, African American parents had a place in the school. They felt comfortable coming and going to the school at their leisure. The faces of teachers and administrators were familiar to them because, in many instances, the teachers and administrators were their friends, neighbors, and fellow church members. Parents could voice their concerns, opinions, and fears about their children's educational achievement, and teachers and administrators listened and responded.

For many African American parents whose children attended segregated schools, parent involvement connoted active participation, collaboration, and co-generative discussions with teachers and administrators. It meant African American parents had some control of the school and school systems that helped shape the character and minds of their children. For example, teaching personnel were accountable to the community, and therefore had to teach effectively if they wanted to maintain their jobs. School performance was relevant to the life experiences and needs of African American children and provided motivation to learn. African American children developed self-worth and dignity through knowledge of their history and culture and through the images provided by community leaders and teachers. African American parents had control through coalition. The schools maintained continual communication with African American parents and developed with these parents a structure that included them in the governing of the schools. African American parents could exert influence to protect their most precious resources, their children. This involvement assisted schools in providing a more relevant education for students.

The point here is that segregation was unequal, unfair, and wrong because the textbooks, equipment, and supplementary materials often were outdated and inferior to what was provided at all-White schools. Despite this, African American schools often implemented a curriculum that reflected high standards and compelled their students to exceed expectations in order to be successful in the "real world." Additionally, African American parents had a sense of value and pride because the African American principals and teachers in these segregated schools made them feel needed, wanted, and included in the business of the school. Derrick Bell (1983) is one of the few policymakers who actually admitted that African American parents should have played a larger part in the *Brown* decision. He apologizes by saying, "There can be no effective schooling for black children without both parental involvement in the educational process and meaningful participation in the school policy making" (p. 575). Lightfoot (1980) reveals that "although the *Brown* decision focused on schooling, it disregarded the development of children and the perspectives of families and communities" (p. 4). Lightfoot further notes that

> Mixing black and white bodies together in the same school and preserving the same relationships and perceptions between schools and families they serve is unlikely to substantially change the structures, roles, and relationships *within* schools that define the quality of the educational process. The nature and distribution of power among schools, families, and communities is a crucial piece of the complex puzzle leading toward educational success for all children. (p. 17, emphasis in original)

Bedtime Stories and Book Reports is the right book at the right time for creating the crucial piece of the puzzle of distributing power among schools, families, communities that Lightfoot refers to. The editors of this text, Catherine Compton-Lilly and Stuart Greene, have been masterful in guiding the development of this book. They have gathered an impressive group of researchers and practitioners to provide insights into working with families in productive and empowering ways. In this highly readable and informative text, the authors offer captivating and intriguing accounts of working with a variety of families in multiple settings. This book is a perfect fit for the Language and Literacy Series as well as a valuable contribution to the field of family engagement. It is extraordinary in its depth and breadth of coverage of important issues and concerns. It will be a useful guide for preservice and experienced teachers, whether they teach at the elementary or secondary level. To say that it is overdue is an understatement. But I'm glad that we finally have this book. Happy reading!

—Patricia A. Edwards
Michigan State University
President, International Reading Association, 2010–2011
Past President, Literacy Research Association
(formerly the National Reading Conference)

REFERENCES

Bell, D. (1983). Learning from our losses: Is school desegregation still feasible in the 1980s? *Phi Delta Kappan, 64*(8), 572–575.

Brown v. Topeka Board of Education, 347 U.S. 483, 1954.

Epstein, J. L. (1987). Parent involvement: State education agencies should lead the way. *Community Education Journal, 14* (4), 4–10.

Lightfoot, S. L. (1980). Families as educators: The forgotten people of *Brown*. In D. Bell (Ed.), *Shades of* Brown: *New perspectives on school desegregation* (pp. 3–19). New York: Teachers College Press.

INTRODUCTION

Stuart Greene
Catherine Compton-Lilly

The U.S. Department of Education issued a report 2 decades ago stating that effective educational methods should regard parents as "children's first and most influential teachers" (Bennett, 1987, p. 107). At that time, the report suggested that parents read to their children frequently and incorporate literacy and numeracy skills into home activities. Policymakers continue to stress the importance of parent involvement and family literacy in addressing the achievement gap between low-income minority students and students in the dominant group. Shortly after taking office in 2009, President Obama addressed the importance of parent involvement and family literacy in a speech to Congress when he reaffirmed a widely held belief that "responsibility for our children's education must begin at home" (p. 1). The assumption the President made in his speech seemed clear enough: Children will flourish when their parents attend school functions, when parents help their children with homework, and when parents take time to read to children.

Our aim in this edited collection of original research is to complicate commonsense notions of parent involvement by listening to parents' stories about how they are involved with their children both in and out of school. All too often, conceptions of parent involvement value the presence of parents in the school building, not parents' awareness of their children's progress in schools, their perceptions of teachers, or their involvement in teaching their children life lessons that extend beyond school achievement. Moreover, portraits of parent involvement are typically brief snapshots limited to isolated moments in time, and parents' voices are often muted. Thus, we present parents' experiences in ways that will help readers understand parents' perceptions of schooling and literacy as well as the models they adopt to interpret what it means to do school. Listening to parents' stories enables teachers to recognize families'

1

funds of knowledge (González, Moll, & Amanti, 2005) and to create curriculum that builds on this knowledge.

Parents bring powerful networks of knowledge, beliefs, and values to educating their children. González and her colleagues (2005) refer to parents' accumulation of experiences in everyday life as "funds of knowledge" that educators can, and should, build upon in order to help children develop as students and as informed citizens. Their research demonstrates that working-class families are competent individuals who have vast bodies of knowledge that often remain invisible to teachers, including experiences within the family, language, literacy, work, parenting, residential history, and other daily activities. By understanding and validating these experiences, teachers can be in a better position to develop innovative strategies for instruction by connecting home and school.

When measured by traditional forms of involvement such as volunteering in children's classrooms, research (Englund, Luckner, Whaley, & Egeland, 2004) affirms a dominant narrative that depicts low-SES parents as less involved in their children's education than higher SES parents. However, in one of the few longitudinal studies of parent involvement, Compton-Lilly (2003, 2007) challenged mainstream discourses that portray urban, low-SES parents as not caring about education by illustrating how their attempts to support children academically relate to and emerge from their difficult social context. Thus their methods of involvement are often different from mainstream methods, and their dedication can be mistaken for apathy and lack of ability.

Of course, the potential for low-income minority students to progress successfully through school is influenced by social histories of economic, cultural, and hardship. Indeed, several problems in urban settings can hinder student learning: inadequate school funding, high teacher-to-student ratios, deteriorating facilities, high teacher and student mobility, and substantial racial and socioeconomic differences between students and staff (e.g., Compton-Lilly, 2003, 2007; Kozol, 2005). Moreover, Brandt (2001) observed that while literacy undeniably has served as an "instrument for more democratic access to learning, political participation, and upward mobility) . . . it has become one of the sharpest tools for stratification and denial of opportunity" (p. 2). When nondominant groups historically have been denied equal or adequate opportunities to acquire literacy, it is vital to identify the conditions that both foster and limit parent involvement and how parent/community/school relationships can converge in support of children's literacy.

A second aim of this volume is to connect parent involvement and family literacy research—two fields that ironically have rarely been brought together. Both fields of study bring into focus the ways that race, class, gender, and history serve as potent factors that shape children's life chances. This book serves to unravel the tensions between these areas of research, particularly in their approaches to studying the local cultures of families, school, and communities.

The fields of parent involvement and family literacy have grown exponentially over the past 2 decades, leading to consternation and conflict over definitions and practices. Some researchers have focused on sharing "approved" practices with nonmainstream families and designing family literacy/involvement programs to ameliorate the uneven learning achievement of specific populations of children (Paratore, 2001; Wasik, 2004). These approaches sometimes have been described as entailing deficit views of children and families (Auerbach, 1995; Cairney, 2002). Other researchers have focused on learning about the involvement and literacy practices that exist within families, taking what I'll term an "additive" rather than a deficit view, by encouraging teachers to recognize and utilize the strengths families bring (Gregory, Long, & Volk, 2004; Haneda, 2006). Differences in the field are confusing to educators and researchers as they continue to work toward supporting families and children with literacy learning.

While educators generally focus on identifying the *right* instructional approaches and the *right* types of school programs, we cannot ignore the broader structural problems in society that create inequality and contribute to the inability of schools and teachers to provide all children with access to resources and opportunities. As Valdés (1996) explains in reference to the challenges faced by first-generation Mexican immigrants, "single-factor explanations of school failure . . . are inadequate and cannot account for the complexity of experience" (p. 29). Few would disagree that good instruction will support student learning, but it is naive to think that an instructional program alone will overcome and address social inequities or that a one-size-fits-all model can ensure school success for children from a range of backgrounds.

SOCIOCULTURAL THEORIES AND INSIGHTS

As cultural, racial, and economic diversity increases in schools and classrooms, it is imperative that we extend our existing understandings of family involvement, home literacy, and the complex relationships that exist among race, class, access, positionality, and power. With this goal in mind, we have conceptualized a book that draws upon sociocultural theories and insights to challenge dominant and deficit discourses about families. The goals of this volume include:

- highlighting the strengths of diverse families,
- revisiting traditional notions of parent involvement,
- understanding the resources parents draw upon to help their children in school,
- exploring historical and contemporary social policies that contextualize the experiences of diverse families,
- identifying those forces in schooling and society that both foster and impede parent involvement, and
- revealing examples of agency and community activism in diverse families.

While grounded in sociocultural theory, this book promises to move beyond theoretical accounts to present examples of community, school, and classroom initiatives that involve families in thoughtful and respectful ways.

Sociocultural perspectives recognize the ways parent involvement and literacy learning relate to people's social and cultural experiences. We focus on two dimensions of those experiences that are particularly relevant to families: literacy practices and critical constructs related to voice, access, and privilege.

Literacy Practices

The term *literacy practices* has assumed a significant place in literacy education. In 2003, Street defined literacy practices as social practices and conceptions related to reading and writing that acknowledge the ways people conceptualize and make sense of literacy events. This revised definition of literacy practices recognizes "the broader cultural conception of particular ways of thinking about and doing reading and writing in cultural contexts" (Street, 2003, p. 79).

David Barton and Mary Hamilton (1998) challenged universal conceptions of literacy competence by highlighting the local nature of literacy practices. They emphasized the ways local literacy practices reflect the uses and purposes of literacy in people's lives. Conceptualizing literacy as sets of practices that reflect local interests and purposes reveals the multifaceted nature of literacy and challenges singular and hegemonic accounts of literacy proficiency. Research in local literacies recognizes the multiple literacies found in diverse homes and communities, and contributes to recognition of the ways certain forms of language and literacy are privileged above others.

Critical Constructs Related to Voice, Access, and Privilege

James Gee (1990) and others (Delpit, 1995; Fairclough, 1995; Ladson-Billings, 1994) are concerned with how language is situated within power-laden cultural, historical, and institutional settings. Specifically, they situate learning within dynamic contexts that recognize language as a social construction that operates within schools and the larger society. Bakhtin (1981) reminds us that language is always produced in interaction with others; social positioning and relative power between speakers are always relevant in determining both what is said and how things are said. It is through power-laden social interactions and participation in particular discourse communities that children acquire social norms and fulfill social expectations (Gee, 1990).

Parent involvement is always situated within power-laden relationships within schools, classrooms, and communities. How parents interact with teachers, how they support their children, how literacy is enacted, what is read and written, and how texts are used, are products of historical understandings about schooling and literacy. Over time particular ways of participating in literacy classrooms are valued over others. Power operates as children's past literacy practices and life experiences are either recognized or dismissed as they enter school and commence formal literacy instruction.

Throughout this book, educators will encounter possibilities for learning about families and working with parents. While we have taken care to introduce our readers to a wide range of families and communities, our primary goal is to provide teachers with examples and tools that they can use in their local communities to learn about the homes lives and literacies of children, develop rich relationships with parents and other family members, and find ways to work alongside families in supporting children as learners.

HOW THE BOOK IS ORGANIZED

This book is divided into two parts: "Research, Issues, and Policies in Parent Involvement" and "Literacy Practices and Experiences: Many Families, Many Literacies, Many Classrooms."

The volume editors each introduce a part and respond to its chapters. Catherine Compton-Lilly, a family literacy researcher, introduces the first part on parent involvement, while Stuart Greene brings his background in parent involvement to the chapters on family literacy in the second part. This cross-disciplinary approach is a first step in connecting these two related, but professionally disparate, areas. In each chapter, the authors underscore the importance of attending to local culture and the value of listening to the voices of family members to complicate reductive conceptions of parent involvement and deficit assumptions about families.

Each chapter closes with a section that addresses how the insights presented in the chapter are relevant to local schools and communities, and could positively affect school practices.

Part I: Research, Issues, and Policies in Parent Involvement

In this part of the book, we explore parent involvement and present activities for connecting homes and schools. We begin with Stuart Greene and his colleague Joyce Long exploring involvement from the perspectives of parents and teachers. Ultimately, their study defines parent involvement by reaffirming the value of understanding parents' beliefs and values, and collaborating with all stakeholders in their child(ren)'s education.

Patricia Snell's chapter, "*Parents* Defining Parent Involvement," extends the work in Greene and Long's chapter to define "involvement" through a participatory action research project. As "promotora" researchers, parents helped to facilitate focus group sessions, analyzed the data, presented the findings to the school community, and reflected on their personal experience throughout the project.

Joyce Long, the author of Chapter 3, "Transformative Change: Parent Involvement as a Process of Becoming," draws upon parents' writing, during a series of parent-involvement workshops, to understand the evolution of their identities as learning with, as well as supporting the learning of, their children.

In the final chapter of Part I, "Parent Involvement with a Purpose: Get the Lead out!" Rebecca Rogers and Darren O'Brien report on the critical literacy practices of a grassroots initiative where parent-activists advocated for lead abatement in local schools. They offer a unique understanding of parent involvement and family literacy—from the perspectives of a parent and a researcher, both citizens concerned with the health and vitality of children.

Part II: Literacy Practices and Experiences: Many Families, Many Literacies, Many Classrooms

In this part of the book, we present a series of family literacy explorations.

In Chapter 5, "Reading Attainment over Time: Following Urban Families," Catherine Compton-Lilly describes how two young readers, Alicia and Peter, simultaneously function within multiple timescales while learning to read as they move through school, from first grade to secondary. She argues that educators and researchers should consider the ways in which children operate within time as they develop literacy and define themselves as readers and writers.

In Chapter 6, "Intergenerational Meaning-Making Between a Mother and Son in Digital Spaces," Tisha Lewis examines how new forms of technology mediate relationships between a mother and son, and how increasingly complex multimodal interactions (Kress & van Leeuwen, 2001) affect home literacy practices and potentially classroom learning.

In Chapter 7, "Talking, Reading, and Writing Lesbian and Gay Families in Classrooms: The Consequences of Different Pedagogical Approaches," Caitlin Ryan analyzes the ways lesbian families are talked, read, and written about in elementary schools, looking closely at two 1st-grade classrooms, each with a different pedagogical approach to including families in the curriculum (or not). She considers different teaching approaches that recognize and respect children's right to come out about their families in ways they choose.

Chapter 8, "God's People Are Strong: Children's Spiritual Literacy Practices," contributes to our understanding of African American family literacy by deepening understandings about spiritual literacy practices. Nadjwa Norton illuminates the ways spiritual children read and write texts with spiritual lenses. Given the legal issues that surround the separation of Church and State, this chapter provides a unique insight into how family culture may be silenced as teachers abide by the need to maintain a secular environment.

Finally, in Chapter 9, *Descubriendo Historias*/Uncovering Stories: The Literacy Worlds of Latino Children and Families," Rosario Ordoñez-Jasis and Susana Flores follow the journey of a group of early childhood educators and researcher/educators who embarked on an inquiry-based project to capture and capitalize on the family literacy practices found in a dynamic, ever-changing, mostly Latino bilingual and bicultural school community—in which they themselves were raised.

POSSIBILITIES FOR CLASSROOMS, SCHOOLS, AND COMMUNITIES

The chapters in this book explore a set of key themes providing readers with possibilities for working with families in their local communities.

- We examine what educators can learn from parents, especially as they work to make classrooms more responsive to the culture, race, class, religious beliefs, and sexual orientation of families. These chapters highlight the importance of teacher inquiry and reflection as a means of learning about families and communities.
- We draw attention to the rich resources that parents and children draw upon and the ways that teachers can build upon these funds of knowledge. The following chapters reveal numerous examples of parental agency and resiliency.
- We explain the value of involving parents in collaborative exchanges that include expertise from multiple constituencies. This text promises to help teachers to become more aware of how pedagogical approaches affect homes.
- We explore information that often is assumed to be neutral or safe, and ask how information can validated in classrooms that are safe for all students.
- We demonstrate that many parents seek to be activists in their children's education. Education is not simply about what children learn or achieve in school—but encompasses the very conditions of the schools they attend.
- We establish the value of teachers providing opportunities for students and their families to participate meaningfully in the processes of constructing school and classroom environments that invite children of all backgrounds and support identities and alliances.
- We illustrate ways to enlist teachers and students in local communities that shape student identities that reflect who they are and what they value.
- We demonstrate ways in which changing communities can foster parent involvement and how parent networks can reach out to other parents.

We believe that the experiences the chapter authors provide, will open a wealth of possibilities for educators to reconsider and explore parent involvement and family literacy in their classrooms, schools, and local communities.

REFERENCES

Auerbach, E. R. (1995). Which way for family literacy intervention or empowerment. In L. M. Morrow (Ed.), *Family literacy: Connections in schools and communi-*

ties (pp. 11–27). Newark, DE: International Reading Association.

Bakhtin, M. M. (1981). The dialogic imagination: Four essays by M. M. Bakhtin. In M. Holquist (Ed.), *Four essays by M. M. Bakhtin* (C. Emerson & M. Holquist, Trans.). Austin: University of Texas Press.

Barton, D., & Hamilton, M. (1998). *Local literacies: Reading and writing in one community.* London: Routledge.

Bennett, W. (1987). Implications for American education. *NASSP Bulletin, 71*(499) 102–108.

Brandt, D. (2001). *Literacy in American lives.* New York: Cambridge University Press.

Cairney, T. (2002). Bridging home and school literacy. *Early Child Development and Care, 172*(2),153–172.

Compton-Lilly, C. (2003). *Reading families: The literate lives of urban children.* New York: Teachers College Press.

Compton-Lilly, C. (2007). *Re-reading families: The literate lives of urban children, four years later.* New York: Teachers College Press.

Delpit, L. (1995). *Other people's children: Cultural conflict in the classroom.* New York: New Press.

Englund, M., Luckner, A., Whaley, G., & Egeland, B. (2004). Children's achievement in early elementary school: Longitudinal effects of parental involvement, expectations, and quality of assistance. *Journal of Educational Psychology, 96*(4), 723–730.

Fairclough, N. (1995). *Critical discourse analysis: The critical study of language.* London & New York: Longman.

Gee, J. P. (1990). *Social linguistics and literacies: Ideologies in discourses.* London: Falmer Press.

González, N., Moll, L., & Amanti, C. (2005). *Funds of knowledge: Theorizing practices in households, communities, and classrooms.* Mahwah, NJ: Erlbaum.

Gregory, E., Long, S., & Volk, D. (2004). *Many pathways to literacy: Young children learning with siblings, grandparents, peers, and communities.* New York: Routledge.

Haneda, M. (2006). Becoming literate in a second language: Connecting home, community, and school literacy practices. *Theory Into Practice, 45*(4), 337–345.

Kozol, J. (2005). *The shame of the nation.* New York: Crown.

Kress, G., & van Leeuwen, T. J. (2001). *Multimodal discourse: The modes and media of contemporary communication.* London: Arnold.

Ladson-Billings, G. (1994). *The dreamkeepers: Successful teachers of African American children.* San Francisco: Jossey-Bass.

Obama, B. (2009). Call for parent involvement. http://blogs.greatschools.net/greatschoolsblog/2009/03/obamas-call-for-parent-involvement.html

Paratore, J. R. (2001). *Opening doors, opening opportunities: Family literacy in an urban community.* Boston: Allyn & Bacon.

Street, B. (2003). What's "new" in new literacy studies? Critical approaches to literacy in theory and practice. *Current Issues in Comparative Education, 5*(2), 77–91.

Valdés, G. (1996). *Con respeto: Bridging the distances between culturally diverse families and schools.* New York: Teachers College Press.

Wasik, B. H. (Ed.). (2004). *Handbook of family literacy.* Mahwah, NJ: Erlbaum.

PART I

Research, Issues, and Policies in Parent Involvement

CATHERINE COMPTON-LILLY

As a researcher who studies literacy in families, it may be unexpected for me to introduce the following chapters on parent involvement. Parent involvement and family literacy generally have occupied separate spaces in the academic literature. Parent involvement has focused on how parents are involved in their children's school experiences. Family literacy casts its attention on the home literacy interactions and experiences of children within families. The common ground between these two fields is not difficult to identify—both fields address families and schooling. Both focus on the role of parents and both share the goal of helping more children to succeed in school.

However, both parent involvement and family literacy practices and policies have been described as grounded in deficit assumptions about parents and families (E. R. Auerbach, 1989, 1995; Cairney, 2003; Gadsden, 2004; Hannon, 1994). For example, E. R. Auerbach (1989) critically analyzed "programs that focus on teaching parents to do school-like activities in the home to assist children with homework" (p. 165). She identified the challenge as learning to understand parents' situations and identifying what educators can do to support the efforts of parents. Auerbach noted a tension between researchers who propose to ameliorate the effects of poverty through perscribed home literacy experiences, and researchers who seek ways to highlight and develop the strengths that children and their family members bring to schools.

In this part, we push the boundaries on traditional parenting possibilities by presenting research that extends parenting conversations in new directions. Stuart Greene, Patricia Snell, Joyce Long, Rebecca

Rogers, and Darren O'Brien interrogate conventional definitions of parent involvement by advocating for parent participatory action research and community-based research initiatives, parents as informal educators, and parents as activists. Each of these initiatives turns a spotlight on the voices and perspectives of parents as well as the knowledge they possess and the power they can wield.

In order to challenge deficit notions of parents and families, authors in the book, and in other venues (D'Emilio, 2002; Ditrano & Silverstein, 2006; Edwards, 2009; Ryan, Kay, Fitzgerald, & Paquette, 2001), have implemented various versions of parent action research. For example, D'Emilio described her work in using the power of story to engage parents with schools. When parents and teachers shared their stories, new relationships and alliances formed that ultimately served students. As D'Emilio explained, this action research project created a foundation for school reform that recognized multiple voices and interests. Other action research projects (Ryan et al., 2001) have paired teachers with parents to focus on the challenges faced by particular students. Some of these action research efforts have involved children with special needs (Ditrano & Silverstein, 2006; Edwards, 2009). Rather than teachers being expected to interpret research findings for dissemination to parents, teachers and parents become co-researchers—working together to collect and analyze data in order to problem-solve the challenges children face in schools.

Parent-involvement research also has begun to attend to parental identities and the ways that parents understand their roles in relation to school. Lightfoot (2004) critiqued traditional views of parent involvement, arguing that parent involvement has multiple meanings and many of these are constrained by the assumptions that often are made about marginalized families. She argued that schools simultaneously have viewed parents as both resources that can be tapped and obstacles to be overcome. These understandings fail to capture the diversity and the complexity of family experiences—and in particular the complex ways parents make sense of their roles and responsibilities.

For example, Auerbach (2002) focused directly on the personal and educational narratives of parents from working–class Latino families. She identified three types of narratives—stories of past struggles with schooling, stories of bureaucratic conflict with schools, and counterstories that challenged official narratives—that could contribute to parent empowerment and redefining family–school relationships. Like Hannon (1994), Auerbach argued that parents and teachers often failed to recognize the extent of the help provided by parents and that even parents who were already involved with their children might need support in recognizing the value of their contribution.

In the following chapters, the issues described above are raised, explored, and extended. Together the authors redefine parent involvement from focusing narrowly on volunteering and helping with homework, to opportunities for participating in forums for action and community research, working directly with children, and engaging in political activism on behalf of children.

REFERENCES

Auerbach, E. R. (1989). Toward a socio-contextual approach to family literacy. *Harvard Educational Review, 59,* 165–181.

Auerbach, E. R. (1995). Which way for family literacy intervention or empowerment. In L. M. Morrow (Ed.), *Family literacy: Connections in schools and communities* (pp. 11–27). Newark, DE: International Reading Association.

Auerbach, S. (2002). "Why do they give the good classes to some and not to others?" Latino parent narratives of struggle in a college access program. *Teachers College Record, 104*(7), 1369–1392.

Cairney, T. (2003). Literacy within family life. In N. Hall, J. Larson, & J. Marsh (Eds.), *Handbook of early childhood literacy* (pp. 85–98). London: Sage.

D'Emilio, B. (2002). Action research on meaningful family involvement by parents, teachers and students: Using the telling strategically. *Penn GSE Perspectives on Urban Education, 1*(2), 1–6.

Ditrano, C. J., & Silverstein, L. B. (2006). Listening to parents' voices: Participatory action research in the schools. *Professional Psychology: Research and Practice, 37*(4), 359–366.

Edwards, B. (2009). Parents and educators working as an action research team. *Educate~, 9*(1), 8–11.

Gadsden, V. L. (2004). Family literacy and culture. In B. H. Wasik (Ed.), *Handbook of family literacy* (pp. 401–425). Mahwah, NJ: Erlbaum.

Hannon, P. (1994). *Literacy, home and school: Research and practice in teaching literacy with parents.* London: Falmer Press.

Lightfoot, D. (2004). "Some parents just don't care": Decoding the meanings of parental involvement in urban schools. *Urban Education, 39*(1), 91–107.

Ryan, A. K., Kay, P. J., Fitzgerald, M., Paquette, S., & Smith, S. (2001, January/February). Kyle: A case study in parent–teacher action research. *Teaching Exceptional Children, 33*(3), pp. 56–61.

CHAPTER 1

FLIPPING THE SCRIPT

Honoring and Supporting Parent Involvement

Stuart Greene
Joyce F. Long

Initiatives designed to foster increased parent involvement have been prevalent in education policy during the past 2 decades. These initiatives have taken on greater urgency since the Clinton administration reauthorized the Elementary and Secondary Education Act (ESEA) and set aside funding to support parent–teacher "compacts" in 1996 (Domina, 2005). In 2002, then Secretary of Education Rod Paige called energetic and enthusiastic involvement from all parents "the most important help of all" in achieving effectiveness for the No Child Left Behind Act (NCLB). Therefore, it is not surprising that NCLB mandates that elementary schools provide "parents with the tools they need to support their children's learning in the home, communicate regularly with families about children's academic progress, provide opportunities for family workshops, and offer parents chances to engage in parent leadership activities at the local site" (Caspe, Lopez, & Wolos, 2006/2007, p. 1).

A growing number of studies have established a positive relationship between parent involvement and student achievement. For example, Greenwood and Hickman (1991) suggest that parent involvement enhances a child's attitude, sense of well-being, and educational aspirations, while also improving grades and readiness for school. Students are also less likely to be placed in special education, repeat a grade, or drop out when their parents are involved (Anderson, 2000). Still, meta-research studying the effects of parent involvement on children's academic progress, or achievement, is inconclusive (Pomerantz, Moorman, & Litwack, 2007) and calls attention to the complex array of factors in children, parents, and communities that affect student learning (see also Prins & Toso, 2008).

15

However, the notion of parent involvement is not well defined. Caspe and her colleagues (2006/2007) underscore the fact that no single factor in what educators refer to as parent involvement is responsible for making a positive difference; instead, multiple factors must occur simultaneously. Specifically, these factors include parent–child relationships at home, the extent to which parents identify with and depend upon communities of adults from different socioeconomic backgrounds, the extent to which parents are a presence at school, and the kinds of support in reading, writing, and math that parents provide for their children. As in Epstein's (1995) model, these factors bring into focus the ways social, cognitive, and affective forms of involvement can influence students' behaviors, sense of competence, and achievement.

COMPLICATING COMMONSENSE VIEWS OF PARENTS AND COMMUNITIES

A number of studies suggest that parents of low SES tend to be less involved in their children's education than higher SES parents, at least when measured by traditional forms of involvement, such as classroom volunteerism and working with children at home. Further, Lareau's (2000) in-depth study reveals that low-SES parents are less likely to supplement curriculum with closely related work at home, to challenge teachers' expertise, and to communicate with other parents about their children's educations.

However, multiple studies also point to the obstacles inadvertently created by school administrators. For example, "mainstream discourses" about reading, which often blame parents for children's reading difficulties, can absolve teachers, schools, and society of responsibility for the educational challenges faced by urban students (Handel, 1999). Discourses like this persist, permitting the rationale that poverty, substandard living conditions, and the like are caused by their victims. Even when schools attempt to reach out to low-income minority parents, too often the focus is solely on the parents and perceived inadequacies on their part (Compton-Lilly, 2003).

Moreover, the tendency in studies of parent involvement is to limit definitions to parents' presence at schools. Yet, as Norton and Ordoñez demonstrate in their respective chapters in this volume, parent involvement can manifest itself in the ways in which parents educate their children as moral, empathic individuals who will live out their lives with integrity, not just in the ways in which they contribute to children's achievement at school. Without a broader conception of parent involvement, it would be easy to ignore just how involved many parents are in helping their children flourish. In keeping with some key themes in this volume, and to more fully realize the context that has shaped parents' views about school, we draw upon parents' voices as they help us understand what they think parent involvement means and the local knowledge in which they live and work.

AN EXAMPLE OF COMMUNITY-BASED RESEARCH

Ultimately, our investigation is motivated not only by what we see as possible limitations in current research, but by the work we have done together as members of a community-based research (CBR) initiative that focuses upon local educational issues (for a brief history of CBR and its efforts, see Strand, Marullo, Cutforth, Stoecker & Donohue, 2003). The group includes teachers and principals from local schools and researchers who have a long history of teaching—in public and private schools. Since the emphasis in CBR is on local knowledge and questions that emerge from conversations with stakeholders in a local context, our ensuing community and faculty dialogue identified a number of issues that we have since refined in preparing for this study: What do we mean by parent involvement? How is it conceptually defined? How has parent involvement been measured in empirical studies? What is the payoff at elementary and middle schools? Have empirical studies identified forms of parent involvement that are most productive? What kinds of incentives increase parent involvement and what obstacles hinder parent involvement?

Our study builds upon a pilot study at a local primary school in collaboration with the same principal with whom we have collaborated on the current study. Specifically, Mangeney (2007) tested Hoover-Dempsey and Sandler's (1995) model of low-SES, parent-involvement decision making. Her findings revealed that the most prominent factors included general opportunities and invitations for involvement, demands on time and energy, and perceptions of personal skills and knowledge. For the most part, all the parents did not believe they had the expertise to challenge teachers' decisions, and most agreed that they did not feel welcome at the school. Some parents seemed to lack a general awareness of what types of activities even constituted parent involvement. For example, when asked what they did to demonstrate involvement in their children's education, parents answered that they took their children to the movies, the mall, and the skating rink. Interestingly, they mentioned helping with homework and reading to children only after being prompted. Moreover, some parents stated that they felt unsure about how to be involved.

The local primary school, Ida B. Wells Primary (a pseudonym), is a neighborhood school in a Midwest city of approximately 110,000 residents. Its 275 students are instructed in 16 K–4 classrooms. Eight additional instructors provide supplemental resources (e.g., art, music, curriculum). Of these 24 teachers, two are male and three are African American. The remaining teachers are Caucasian females. Collectively, they have been at the school for an average of 7 years, but the range of teaching experience extends from 1 year to 27 years.

Since 86% of its students qualified for free lunch in 2005–06, the school is categorized as a Title I school. Data for the 2006–07 school year (when this study was conducted) estimate the following racial composition: 48% Black, 21% Hispanic, 15% White, 12% multiracial, and 4% Asian. According to the 2000 Census, 14.2% of families living in the census block groups that the school serves live below poverty. Furthermore, 30.4% of children under 18 in the main census tract within the school's boundaries live in poverty. Data on educational attainment show that roughly 75% and 25% of the population over age 25 have graduated high school and college, respectively. Although these data hint at the low SES of the surrounding community, they are also somewhat misleading since the neighborhood includes professional families, many of whom work at a local university. However, very few children whose families are associated with the university actually attend the school.

The No Child Left Behind Report Card for Ida B. Wells from 2004–2007 showed passing rates below both district and state rates in every category except one. (The school's passing rate in math for paid-lunch students was 4 percentage points higher than the district rate.) Some of the most disconcerting statistics include a 26% passing rate in math for African American students, compared with 42% in the district and 45% in the state; a 31% passing rate in English/language arts (LA) for Hispanic students compared with 44% in the district and 54% in the state; and a 0% passing rate in English/LA for special education students.

Moreover, large gaps exist between free-lunch and paid-lunch students and between minority and White students. For example, 80% and 70% of paid-lunch students passed math and English/LA, respectively, while only 33% and 36% of free-lunch students passed these tests. Moreover, only 32.4% of students at Ida B. Wells passed both the English/LA and math portions of the state standardized test in the 2006–07 school year, compared with 64.2% statewide.

With the principal of the school, we organized a series of workshops with parents to identify the ways in which parents perceived what it meant to be involved, to consider ways that they could build upon the things they were already doing, and to enter into a sustained conversation with teachers, so that they could work together as partners to ensure that children were flourishing. Altogether, 11 parents consistently attended the workshops—seven females and four males, with an average age of 36. Five had completed high school; two more had passed their GED equivalency exams. Demographically, one was Caucasian, one Latino, and nine were either African American or African American mix. Parents' ethnic backgrounds represented the community's demographics. At the outset, three identified themselves as being married—although one couple wed midway through the project.

A NOTE ON METHODS

We examined parents' perceptions about what it meant to be involved in their children's education by collecting life histories. We asked parents about their backgrounds (Can you tell me about the neighborhood where you live now? How is it the same as or different from the neighborhood where you grew up?) and their education (How much schooling did your grandparents have? What about your parents? Can you tell me a story about your education, something that stands out or that you remember at any point in your education?).

One week after the interviews, we began a series of 10 workshops. At the first meeting, each parent completed a survey designed to gather information about how parents feel about the school their children attend (e.g., whether they feel welcome), the extent to which parents feel that teachers invite them to be involved, and what they need in order to support their children's learning (Epstein & Salinas, 1993). In addition to completing the survey, each parent participated in a focus group, which directly focused on their perspectives about parent involvement (Fine & Weis, 1998): "How involved are you in your child's education? Would you like to be more involved? What keeps you from being involved?" A second informal focus group was conducted following the workshops' conclusion to revisit parents' definitions of parent involvement and obtain specific examples of how they were involved in their children's schoolwork.

Finally, we asked the schools' classroom teachers and resource instructors to complete a teacher version of the same survey, asking teachers to judge their school's role in supporting involvement and to describe activities they themselves employed for engaging parents in their classrooms. In addition, we asked the teachers about their definitions of parent involvement, ways to encourage involvement, and formats used to communicate with parents (e.g., newsletters, phone calls, home visits).

WHAT WE CAN LEARN FROM PARENTS
ABOUT PARENT INVOLVEMENT

In general, parents not only described their relationships with children as being close, but were able to cite examples of activities they shared together that confirmed the depth of their affection for their children. Parents spoke of playing baseball or basketball together, going fishing, redecorating the child's bedroom, playing video games, going to the park, skating, watching movies—whatever the child felt like doing. One parent proudly boasted of his daughter's writing three stories about her friendship with her father, and another shared that he took his son to work frequently.

In addition to stories about activities they shared together, parents also spoke of their children's weaknesses and strengths, indicating they knew the personalities of their children, and how children differed from one another. Boys frequently were referred to as being active and needing to play outside, because they have "energy to burn, apparently." Other children were described as liking computers, reading, or arts and crafts. One parent went out of her way to support her daughter's interests:

> So I just encourage that and she might be a home interior decorator, I don't know. So, anything that's artsy-crafty I try to buy that for her. And just to keep her encouraged in that area. You know, maybe she'll be a jewelry designer, who knows.

Although the focus of our project was on parent involvement with school, these limited references in the data indicate that parents enjoy their children and are intent on developing warm relationships with them in their homes. Even when employment demands forced limits on the amount of contact one parent might have with children, we heard many spontaneous stories that demonstrated the extent to which both parents coordinated their schedules so that children generally were supervised and cared for.

PARENT INVOLVEMENT AT HOME

One parent, Lamont, captured others' concerns when he explained that he is "very involved" with his son: "You know, when I'm not working on my second job, when I'm always, when he comes straight home from school, homework first. I make sure he do that before he go outside, or he do anything, you know, and he take off his coat, I say homework, homework, homework. You know, to let him know that's instilled in his mind, homework. Get that work done, make sure it's right." Lamont creates a structure of expectations for his son after school, so that he gets right to work.

This is a significant concern for all of the parents, who expressed concern over the number of distractions (e.g., computer games, television, and bicycles) that interfere with children's focus on schoolwork. They uniformly agreed that children, after a full day of school, would much rather engage in other activities than attend to homework. Like other parents, Lamont tries to let his son figure out ways to do his work independently. Thus, he just monitors his son's progress. "What I do now is let him do it himself, and then I check it and see if it's done right. Most time it is done right." Similarly, Beth explains that she sits all of her children down at the dining room table, "and if it gets to the point where nobody can figure it out, which is rare, then, you know . . . I do that, but as far as the homework helping goes, . . . I have them do it with each other a lot more. And I think that helps 'em, you know, to just look out for one another." Still, parents often gave some direct instruction when helping with homework, as was the case for Carol: "Sometimes I have to, you know, [*inaudible*] and show him words and that he missed and stuff like that, but he, you know, instill in him homework, you know. Before you go outside and play, homework."

Many parents talked about "maintaining high expectations." For example, Devon reflected on his daughter's interest in watching medical shows and has told her that she should consider being a doctor. Moreover, because he works as security guard at a local university, he makes sure that she comes to the university with him as often as possible. Although Beth and Devon have made it clear to their children that they are expected to attend college, presurvey data revealed that only 78% of the parents frequently emphasized that school is important. By the end of the workshops, data from the survey revealed that nearly all of the parents stressed the value of school in their conversations with their children.

Parents placed considerable emphasis on who their children are as learners, which was reflected in students' apparent interests and desires. Devon explained, "Whatever they do in the computer lab—that's what mine likes—working in the computer lab. Whatever stuff they have them doing, you know, she likes. She loves being on the computer." Therese also emphasized the need to "find out what your kid really likes, what he really likes in school. If it's math, reading, English, or art, whatever. You have to find that out, in fact, like I find out my little boy, he loves math but, you know, a whole lot so sometimes I take him to my job." Unfortunately, Therese continued by conveying that she is not always certain that teachers know what the children are interested in and that, to teach effectively, teachers need to ask both the parents and the children.

Parents also described examples in which they intentionally created and participated in interactive instructional lessons with their children to help them learn a variety of academic skills. Examples included playing store with a cash register so children would learn how to estimate the price of items in the home and be able to give correct change. Indeed, one parent described learning as an "everyday process" that could be incorporated in play:

> I don't care who you are, how old you are, you learn something
> new every day, and it can either be really exciting for you to
> learn, or it could be boring and then the kids are like, you know,
> they're really not excited. I mean, you know, you can play to
> learn.

Some parents also conducted spelling bees in which children could earn prizes purchased from the local dollar store. In both examples, parents demonstrate the ways play can scaffold learning.

Another parent related stories of taking his child to his job site and letting him use the cash register there. This same parent, whom we later realized was only functionally literate, took his son grocery shopping, let him pick out the kind of food he liked, and then gave him a $100 bill to cover the total amount. The father had prearranged with the cashier to give back incorrect change, so when the child was asked to figure out how much money he was supposed to receive, he had to perform math calculations and excercise conflict resolution skills in talking to the cashier. After sharing this example, the parent also suggested that learning could be improved if involved adults found out what children really liked and enjoyed. Readily admitting that his son had problems with math at the beginning of the year, he "found the fun part of him," and practiced those skills so now "he's doing pretty good in math." When you find the fun part of it, he claimed, "they catch on real quick, you know, after awhile." Apparently these parents recognized the need for reinforcing academic skills in their children and assumed they could design practical, innovative, and effective ways to help them learn without seeking professional input.

TEACHERS' DEFINITIONS OF PARENT INVOLVEMENT

Teachers' responses were very similar when asked to define what they meant by parent involvement and the extent to which they had invited parents to participate in school activities (both formal and informal). Although teachers' definitions of parent involvement did include occasional references to experiences at home "with the fun things and also the academics," their expectations centered primarily on two factors traditionally noted by researchers: (1) communicating with teachers, and (2) participating in school events (parent–teacher conferences, visiting the classroom, performances, field trips, volunteering). Interestingly, few teachers personally knew any parents who helped at the school. This difference in definitions of parent involvement helps explain some significant gaps in parents' and teachers' thinking about what it means to be involved in children's education.

In interviews, most teachers suggested that parents were unresponsive; however, findings indicate that there could be mismatches between teachers' expectations and parents' understanding of how to respond to phone calls or letters sent home. After discovering that his daughter had not completed seven assignments, one parent solved the "problem" by sitting down with her and showing her how to do the assignments.

> I do get the notes, you know, but they're doing better and we know, we stay on 'em about their school, I mean we stay on 'em, checking homework daily and whatever, and, you know, I ask 'em, "How you doing? You have any problems, what is it?" Just like my daughter brought home some homework and I was looking at it this morning and she had missed like seven—she said these are new problems that are hard. I said, well I'll go through this, and then we'll pick out the problem that you're having a hard time with and then I'll make up some problems for you to do when I'm off Wednesday and Thursday and we'll go through 'em and get you going good on 'em. So, you know, I stay on 'em.

On the one hand, this parent feels like he is following through with his responsibility as a supportive parent. On the other hand, the teacher was probably frustrated because her student missed numerous assignments, but the parent never replied to her attempts to communicate with him.

Another teacher observed that the challenges to ongoing communication and participation are quite real and reflect the larger socioeconomic concerns that face the urban poor: "Mostly the parents that I wanted to see were the ones that didn't come in. And a lot of times it's difficult to contact them, there's not a working telephone or, you know, no other way to get hold of them." Similarly, teachers noted that many of their students were in single-parent families where the parent worked at least two jobs, did not have transportation, and dealt with language barriers.

POSSIBILITIES FOR YOUR CLASSROOM, SCHOOL, AND COMMUNITY

Most telling in our study was that teachers emphasized parents' lack of participation in formal and informal activities at school, and stressed their attempts to communicate information to parents. In contrast, parents focused on the ways they helped children with homework, but rarely addressed their participation at school or communication with teachers and administrators. Even if teachers believe they are communicating *to* parents, communication *with* parents does not necessarily occur. In fact, although they do not know that they agree, both parents and teachers believe that meaningful dialogue is absent from their contact. Until each group begins to talk to, know, and understand the other, it is virtually impossible for a parent–school partnership to form.

Our research indicates that parents need to realize that their role at school is significant. Yet history shows us how disempowered and diminished low-income parents can be within a school. There are many painful reminders that invisible forces impede low-income urban parents from coming to the schoolhouse door, ranging from Kozol's (1965) chronicle of parent protest in *Death at an Early Age* when the superintendent of schools in Boston referred to parents as "stains" in the community, to Purcell-Gates's (1995) description 30 years later of how parents are overlooked or silenced by teachers and administrators. These vestiges of unfortunate legacies suggest that initiatives must totally redefine what is possible and then their implementation must be actively supported until mature connections are developed.

Despite the public's belief that low-income minority parents are not invested in their children's education, our study supports other research results (e.g., Compton-Lilly, 2003), demonstrating that parents not only are interested in their children's schooling, but also want to participate in supporting them. However, it also appears that parents in our study have been unaware of the fact that teachers and administrators have expectations of them that remain unfulfilled.

One teacher aptly characterized the problem of encouraging increased parent involvement at school as a "block," and pointed out that neither parents nor teachers know how to come together to help students. This teacher helps to pinpoint one of the real challenges before us, and the extent to which parent involvement needs to be seen as a reciprocal partnership that unites parents and teachers.

There's this block as far as, I think in general, across the United States, that the parents are on one side and the teacher and the school is on the other side. But everybody really wants the same thing. It's just how to come together to reach that goal. . . . And, I think neither side really knows how to come about that, and I see the, it being more of an outreach from the school side than the parents' side, because the parents are in a different place. They don't have as much capability to plan things out. And I think when some parents want to get involved, it's not so readily acceptable.

As this teacher suggests, schools need to reach out to parents. And teachers must listen to parents, especially if they understand that they need to reach out to parents by encouraging parent input and volunteerism.

Parents are not always cognizant of their potential role. They simply and implicitly trust teachers to provide their children with the formal skills and content knowledge equated with learning. Although they want their children to receive a good education, they do not view themselves as educators. Not until the last workshop, when parents were given their children's standardized test scores for a second time, did they begin to realize that their children were not doing well at all. Their children's academic performance was below par, and the parents realized that they needed to play a more active role in their children's education.

Whether or not parents and schools can forge partnerships may very well be a function of how fluid schools and their communities become. Parents can and are willing to change, as our data indicate, and to become more involved in their children's education. But schools must change, especially their tendency to isolate both teachers and students from the wealth of knowledge in local communities. And this will mean listening to parents' stories, understanding who they and their children are, and expanding a curriculum that bridges the school and community. The implications can be powerful when parents see that schools are committed to them and build on what they know. But invitations to participate must be authentic, not just rhetorical. Parents and teachers need spaces where they can talk about the purpose of education and the value of different curricula for helping children flourish. Here parents and teachers can begin to connect the process of teaching and learning to local communities, where teaching and learning occur all the time.

REFERENCES

Anderson, S. (2000). How parental involvement makes a difference in reading achievement. *Reading Improvement, 37*, 61–86.

Caspe, M., Lopez, M., & Wolos, C. (2006/2007). *Family involvement in elementary school children's education.* Cambridge, MA: Harvard Family Research Project.

Compton-Lilly, C. (2003). *Reading families: The literate lives of urban children.* New York: Teachers College Press.

Domina, T. (2005). Leveling the home advantage: Assessing the effectiveness of parental involvement in elementary school. *Sociology of Education, 78,* 233–249.

Epstein, J. L. (1995). School/family/community partnerships: Caring for the children we share. *Phi Delta Kappan, 76*(9), 701–712.

Epstein, J. L., & Salinas, K. C. (1993). *School and family Partnerships: Surveys and summaries.* Baltimore: Center on Families, Communities, Schools, and Children's Learning.

Fine, M., & Weis, L. (1998). *The unknown city: The lives of poor and working-class young adults.* Boston, MA: Beacon Press.

Greenwood, G., & Hickman, C. (1991). Research and practice in parent involvement: Implications for teacher education. *Elementary School Journal, 91,* 279–288.

Handel, R. (1999). *Building family literacy in an urban community.* New York: Teachers College Press.

Hoover-Dempsey, K., & Sandler, H. (1995). Parental involvement in children's education: Why does it make a difference? *Teachers College Record, 97,* 310–331.

Kozol, J. (1985). *Death at an early age: The destruction of the hearts and minds of Negro children in the Boston public schools.* New York: New American Library.

Lareau, A. (2000). *Home advantage: Social class and parental intervention in elementary education* (2nd ed.). Lanham, MD: Rowman & Littlefield.

Mangeney, J. (November 2007). *Understanding under-involvement: The involvement decisions of motivated, low-SES parents.* New York: National Council of Teachers of English.

Pomerantz, E. M., Moorman, E. A., & Litwack, S. D. (2007). The how, whom, and why of parents' involvement in children's academic lives: More is not always better. *Review of Educational Research, 77*(3), 373–410.

Prins, E., & Toso, B. (2008). Defining and measuring parenting for educational success: A critical discourse analysis of the Parent Education Profile. *American Educational Research Journal, 45,* 555–596.

Purcell-Gates, V. (1995). *Other people's words: The cycle of low literacy.* Cambridge, MA: Harvard University Press.

Strand, K., Marullo, S., Cutforth, N., Stoecker, R., & Donohue, P. (2003). *Community-based research and higher education.* San Francisco: Jossey-Bass.

A Response to Chapter 1

Catherine Compton-Lilly

Greene and Long document the lessons that educators can learn from parents, highlighting the dreams and concerns parents have about their children and the challenges they encounter when dealing with schools and teachers. They show teachers and researchers how they can interview parents and use their reported life histories to design workshops that cater to parents' concerns.

Educators tend to define parent involvement in traditional ways—as communicating with teachers and participating in school events. However, discussions with parents revealed a much broader range of activities. Greene and Long describe parents playing sports and video games, fishing, redecorating, going to parks, and skating with their children. While these are not the traditional indicators of parent involvement that schools might expect, they are significant and must be recognized as contributing to strong foundations upon which school learning can be constructed. Greene and Long note that "parent involvement can manifest itself in the ways in which parents educate their children as moral, empathic individuals who will live out their lives with integrity" (p. 10).

By revealing the vast range of activities that parents share with children, Greene and Long provide readers with data that challenge deficit models of parents and can begin to mend the gap between parents and teachers and thus address some of the tensions that often accompany school and home relationships.

However, Greene and Long raise one more important point. They remind readers that just as teachers often carry negative assumptions about parents, parents are often unaware of their own potential and fail to recognize the significant role they play in their children's educational lives. Rather than challenging teachers' judgment, parents "simply and implicitly trust teachers to provide their children with the formal skills and content knowledge" (p. 27). While efforts to support parents often privilege dominant perspectives and practices, rejecting the strengths that families possess, Greene and Long use research as a means to empower parents, validate their contributions to schooling, and address local educational issues.

In Chapter 2, Patricia Snell also explores the obstacles faced by parents who might want to be more involved with schools. She employs a participatory action research project to document the challenges parents face and to explain the various stances parent take toward becoming engaged.

Then, in Chapter 3, Long returns to the study presented in Chapter 1. Rather than focusing on the lessons researchers and educators can learn from parents, Long highlights how parent involvement can facilitate the development of parental academic identities that support parents as educators in their own homes.

CHAPTER 2

PARENTS DEFINING
PARENT INVOLVEMENT

Patricia Snell

"Now I know how to talk to teachers."
"I always attend meetings and am part of the parent group."
"I learned from other parents' advice."
"I understand more about the norms of the school."
"I am prepared to be involved in the school. I have more power, more action."
—Parent Promotora Researchers

Parent involvement within schools can lead toward measurable school improvement outcomes. However, many struggling schools do not see their parents as being regularly involved in schools. As discussed by Greene and Long in the previous chapter, commonsense notions often paint low-income and minority parents as particularly uninterested or unengaged in their children's education. In this chapter, I ask: How might schools better connect with low-income and minority families and work toward further involving them in schools?

As described in Chapter 1, understanding parents' existing definitions of involvement is key to increasing parent involvement with schools. However, it is also essential that educators and researchers attend to the barriers that parents face as they strive to become involved. Taking a collaborative approach not only acknowledges parents' current efforts but actually can increase their engagement within the school by helping them to overcome barriers that often separate low-income and minority parents from their children's school environments. Collaboration must involve efforts to hear parents' voices and seek ways to help them feel welcomed in schools.

This chapter examines the implementation of a particular type of research investigation called participatory action research, or PAR. PAR designs are meant specifically to investigate ways of hearing from people who often are marginalized by mainstream society. Employing PAR as a parent-involvement strategy allows parents to participate in meaningful ways in defining the very involvement that they are asked to perform. In this case, the project focused on a school thought to have low parent involvement. At the start of the project, parents appeared to be disengaged from the school, although the school had implemented several unsuccessful efforts to involve more parents. Upon completion of the project, parents described their own transformation from having participated in the PAR process.

COMPLICATING COMMONSENSE VIEWS OF PARENTS AND COMMUNITIES

Many teachers, school administrators, and researchers tend to define the term "parent involvement" as consisting of parental activities *within* school buildings (e.g., Chapman, McManus, & Vaden-Kiernan, 2005; Griffith, 1996; Okpala, Okpala, & Smith, 2001). By these definitions, low-income parents are rated as less involved than higher income parents. Likewise, Hispanic and African American parents typically are rated as less involved than White parents (Chapman et al., 2005).

However, researchers have questioned this picture, resulting in different evaluations of parent involvement. Some find that Hispanic and African American parents participate in education as much as or more than White parents (Ho Sui-Chu & Willms, 1996). Others find that parents from different economic backgrounds do not necessarily participate more or less, but rather hold distinct understandings of parenting roles and purposes (e.g., Lareau 2003). These views result in different models of parenting that stress some activities over others, with implications for parent-involvement definitions.

Because schools typically have not involved parents in defining parent involvement and identifying the barriers that parents actually face (Trumbull, Rothstein-Fisch, & Hernandez, 2003), many existing understandings of the concept explain low involvement through assumed parental boundaries, such as lack of interest, time, child care, language, and transportation (Christenson, 2003). Including more parental voices in defining involvement reveals other barriers, including educator and institutional barriers, related to the limited time available to school personnel, stereotypic views of families, and unwelcoming school environments (Christenson, 2003).

Despite this important gap in our understanding of parent involvement, only a handful of researchers have investigated how community members and parents can be engaged in schools to define their own involvement (Clark et al., 2003; Cooper & Christie, 2005; Ho, 2002). Investigations need to explore the ways in which definitions of parent involvement may hinder low-income and minority parents from becoming more engaged. Making exchanges more collaborative means including expertise from all parties and bringing to the table those who, ironically, have been most left out of the parent-involvement conversation—parents.

A NOTE ON METHODS

Participatory action research is a method that constructs research as a process of empowerment, focused on including the voices of the most marginalized by validating their contributions to understanding the situation (Sohng, 1995). The goal for this study was to include those most disenfranchised by traditional parent-involvement definitions—the parents—in defining their own engagement. The middle school studied was located in a large urban area and served a majority Latino/a population and minority African American population. The vast majority (more than 90%) of the students received free or reduced lunch, and nearly 20% of the students were English-language learners.

An important step in the research process was to identify "promotora" researchers. This is a term, literally meaning promoter, that refers to community members involved in the project as leaders facilitating the process (Giblin, 1989; Lukes, 2003; Ramos, May, & Ramos, 2001). In this study, four parents, three monolingual Spanish-speaking women who self-identified as Mexicana and one English-speaking woman who self-identified as Black American, became promotora researchers. These researchers were trained, involved in the research design, and relied upon to recruit parents to participate in the study. A total of 23 parents participated in four focus group sessions, held during multiple times, with child care provided. See Snell, Miguel, and East (2009) for additional information on study methods.

FAMILY VOICES: CONTEXTUALIZING INVOLVEMENT

One of the findings of this study is that parents described a number of general themes that help to explain barriers to parent involvement from their perspective. These issues help to contextualize parent involvement in a way that allows schools and teachers to better meet the parents where they are, first, and then begin to find ways to further involve parents. One of the major themes described by parents is difficult community issues that complicate and interfere with their school involvement. The stories shared by parents contained numerous references to mobility, lack of male role models, domestic violence, lack of safety in the neighborhood, and trouble with the law. They discussed the impact this had on their children by causing decreased school performance, trouble adapting, cultural conflicts as children adjusted to new neighborhood dynamics, drug and alcohol use, and school, family, and neighborhood violence. It was clear from these stories that simply keeping their children safe enough to attend school was one of the major tasks that parents were engaged in with their children.

Another main theme of the groups was a disconnect between families and the school. Many parents reported feeling that they did not know what was going on at the school or were confused about school rules and policies. They explained that the school communicated with them primarily by sending letters home with the children, but the children did not always bring these papers to them. Parents voiced that they would like the school to make other efforts to communicate with them, and many shared stories of memorable moments when teachers were able to contact them by phone to talk about their child's progress.

The Hispanic and African American parents also noted cultural differences and experiences of racial discrimination. They noted differences in the school's and parents' approaches to authority figures and commented that they often did not want to teach their children to approach authority figures in the way the school seemed to desire. Parents who described these cultural differences had not previously thought this was an issue they could address with the school and only now were able to share the experiences due to the feeling of support offered by the shared parental setting.

Although parents expressed a number of difficulties and disconnects in communication between home and school, they also described a number of positive and memorable experiences with teachers. They felt empathy for the teaching staff, with overcrowded classrooms and less knowledge of each individual child than the parents had. They tended to see themselves as trying to help out teachers and be involved with the school primarily through activities at home. Rather than focusing on participating in activities within the school, as the studies previously discussed did, parents tended to focus on those activities they were involved in at home, which they believed had results within the school. These activities included supporting and encouraging children, helping with homework, reading to them, communicating with them, teaching them to be respectful, responding to student performance, and disciplining children for behaviors at school. They specifically mentioned family literacy activities, such as working with their children on reading difficulties, as part of their school involvement. While teachers typically may perceive these actions to be part of the family environment and not consider them to be a direct form of parent involvement in schools, parents clearly identified these actions as ways that they were involved with the school.

TYPES OF PARENT-INVOLVEMENT STRATEGIES

This study revealed four different types of parent-engagement strategies related to the ways parents described themselves and their peers. After listening to the reasons parents listed for why they became involved, why they were previously uninvolved, and why they thought other parents were or were not involved, the following patterns emerged. Some parents were described as having low knowledge of the need to act and low intention to act. The parents who were interviewed reported that these parents simply could not be involved at that time in their lives. Perhaps they were experiencing too many of the obstacles described earlier; they were too busy with work, or they were physically unable. Regardless, the parents who were interviewed believed that teachers simply could not engage these parents at that time. However, it is important for teachers to recognize the difference between this group and other groups of parents. It is equally important for teachers to understand that these descriptions can overlap.

A second group of parents were identified as having the potential to become engaged if involvement activities were linked directly to their self-interests. These parents had significant potential for becoming involved but were low in terms of their willingness to act on their values. If school activities directly benefited these parents or their children, parents would be likely to become involved. Encouraging these parents to become involved thus required that teachers identify the parents' self-interests and find ways to respond to their needs. The typical self-interests of this group were described as: (1) cash and other funding, (2) support from other parents, (3) extra credit for their children, (4) entertainment, and (5) job skills. In other words, to engage parents, schools and teachers could offer cash and other prize raffles, give extra credit to students whose parents participated, and provide other tangible rewards for participation. Parents who were interviewed noted that over time these strategies would encourage parents to become engaged and that they might adopt characteristics of other types of parents, especially if they began to value intrinsic rewards for their participation.

A third group of parents was willing to act on values for the betterment of others but lacked the information necessary to do so. These parents did not need self-interest motivations for becoming involved, but rather needed additional sources of information and support. Strategies for involving parents who fell into this third group required a focus on communication and outreach. The parents who were interviewed described reaching these parents through both mass and personal communication, direct invitations to specific events, lists of opportunities for involvement, recruitment by other parents, and helping these parents to access people and school resources to gain more information about becoming involved.

Finally, a fourth group of parents appeared willing and able to act on their values for the betterment of others. The parents who were interviewed described these parents as 100% committed and needing only minor efforts to feel welcomed, informed, and recognized. These parents were already attending parent events and regularly keeping in touch with the school. They required minimal effort to foster engagement; instead they required focused efforts to support their ongoing engagement. Regularly honoring parents for their participation and directly expressing gratitude for their involvement were all these parents needed to sustain their involvement. This latter group of parents often could be relied on to act as parent-leaders, and they enjoyed their engagement more if they were given the opportunity to lead. Basically, all teachers had to do with this group was ask, say thank you, and continue to keep them informed of needs and opportunities.

One significant implication of this study is the realization that parents are not a unified group and are not involved with schools for a variety of reasons. It is natural for teachers to wish that all parents were completely committed, but they simply are not. Being such a parent is likely grounded in a host of previous experiences and leadership opportunities that only some parents are privileged enough to enjoy. However, recognizing that parents do not meet these expectations does not mean that they necessarily fit the category of uninvolved parents. This insight allows teachers to consider the ways in which parents might be encouraged to work toward an "ideal" as they become increasingly involved with school initiatives. Targeting strategies to each type of parent group allows more effort to be spent on parents who have the greatest potential. It can also result in the creation of different types of activities, which may increase the number of parents who ultimately become involved. This approach also allows teachers to rely most heavily on the most involved parents to assist in recruiting other parents. In the end, none of these categories are permanent, and efforts should be made to revisit all parental types and to provide opportunities for parents to move from one group to another.

PARENT-INVOLVEMENT TRANSFORMATION

Arguably the most important part of the PAR process lies in the transformation that occurs with participating parents. Hearing and understanding their perspectives about parent involvement proved to be a useful tool for further engaging parents with the school. In other words, the process of acknowledging the activities that parents were already engaged in and their perceptions of parent involvement created a parent–school connection that encouraged parents to become further involved. One crucial way this occurred was through the action steps taken as part of the PAR process.

After contributing their input in the focus groups, parents were asked to participate in a number of community events. Promotora researchers became leaders in the school and presented the study results to other parents, teachers, school administrators, and community members. Figure 2.1 summarizes the promotora researcher focus group reflections on their transformations from these experiences. Parents described themselves as moving from facing a number of obstacles to parent involvement—including fear, shame, language problems, a lack of empowerment and interest, unfamiliarity, feelings of being unwelcome—to further involvement in the school, including talking with teachers, attending meetings, feeling more knowledgeable about school procedures, visiting the school regularly, and connecting more with people in the school. The promotora researchers went on to form and participate in a parent-engagement leadership group that met with teachers to talk about ways of implementing suggestions raised during this study. As a first step, the parent-leaders created the following vision statement for involvement: "Teachers, students, parents, and community members all work together to help students reach goals that they thought were unreachable. Everyone in the school community will demonstrate respect for him or herself and each other."

POSSIBILITIES FOR YOUR CLASSROOM, SCHOOL, AND COMMUNITY

For the parents involved in this study, the key to their further involvement within the school was that their perspective be amply heard and responded to by school representatives. For schools to engage low-income and minority parents, it is important for the presence of risk factors in family environments to be acknowledged. Educators must recognize the toll that crisis, mobility, and transition can take on the lives of children

FIGURE 2.1. Parent Self-Described Transformation

Before Involvement in PAR Process:	After Involvement in PAR Process:
Fear and shame to talk with teachers. Language barriers. Not involved in the school. Sometimes attended meetings. Impotent to change school. Ignorant of the system/culture. Desire to be involved, volunteer, and learn more about the school. Less interested in educational programs and never invited to program for helping other parents. Did not know people in the school. Inexperienced with kids at this age. Unfamiliar with cultures within school. Did not know how to be involved at the middle school level. Before was involved for the children.	Ability to talk with teachers. Access to translation. Always attend meetings/groups. Knowledge of school and cultural norms. Understanding of parent rights. Participate and take action here. Skills to help with homework. New parenting strategies. Learned about different cultures. Know people in the school. Ability to involve and aid other parents. Held parent meeting at house. Increased personal goals. Respected as a leader/example. Prepared for involvement in school. Now involved for the parents/school.

and families. Parents clearly stated that they had observed the negative effects these difficult situations had on their children's grades and attendance. Poverty is a daily reality for many families. Although the family environment need not become an excuse for poor performance, attendance, or behavior by children, the first step to effectively engaging parents is to create avenues for discussion and to acknowledge the difficulties in their lives without blame or judgment. Identifying the four types of parent involvement provides a way to do this.

The second step is to work to bridge the gap between the home and school environments. In today's globalized and rapidly changing society, parents cannot be assumed to know the norms and procedures of the school system. Thus, it is the school's role to help parents navigate the differences between the current educational system and that of their childhood. Schools and families can work together to define the purpose of education, acknowledging the value in both sets of visions. One effective means to foster these discussions is to address safety in the school and neighborhood. This is a common and prevalent concern for all involved and it provides an avenue for bringing teachers and parents together.

To deepen parent involvement within the school, the next step is for school personnel to recognize that home steps lead to school results. Traditional definitions of parent involvement tend to value only those efforts by parents that take place within the physical confines of the school. Yet this study shows that most of what parents describe as their support of their children's education occurs at home. As these home activities have an impact on school achievement, attendance, and behavior, it is crucial for schools to find ways to strengthen and support these existing efforts. School personnel first can ask about and understand what strategies parents currently are employing, and then collaborate on ways to further them. The critical idea here is that teachers position themselves as facilitating existing parent strategies first, then invite further school involvement.

Another crucial aspect of the process was the parental transformation that occurred as a result of the project itself. In describing their perspective and helping the school understand their varying needs, parents increased their impact as leaders at the school. In other words, teachers simply hearing and providing space to discuss these issues created a change in involvement. Trust and the ability to relate with other parents were an important aspect of parental willingness to participate. The process of respectful exchange embedded in this PAR approach acted as a parent-involvement strategy. This model shows that teachers can employ relatively simple processes for listening to parents, which, even within one school year, can increase parent engagement in schools.

REFERENCES

Chapman, C., McManus, J., & Vaden-Kiernan, N. (2005). *Parent and family involvement in education: 2002–03*. Washington, DC: National Center for Education Statistics.

Christenson, S. (2003). The family–school partnership: An opportunity to promote the learning competence of all students. *School Psychology Quarterly, 18*(4), 454–482.

Clark, M., Cary, S., Diemert, G., Ceballos, R., Sifuentes, M., Atteberry, I., Vue, F., & Trieu, S. (2003). Involving communities in community assessment. *Public Health Nursing, 20*(6), 456–463.

Cooper, C., & Christie, C. (2005). Evaluating parent empowerment: A look at the potential of social justice evaluation in education. *Teachers College Record, 107*(10), 2248–2274.

Giblin, P. (1989). Effective utilization and evaluation of indigenous health care workers. *Public Health Reports, 104*, 361–368.

Griffith, J. (1996). Relation of parent involvement, empowerment, and school traits to student academic performance. *Journal of Educational Research, 90*(1), 33–41.

Ho, B. (2002). Application of participatory action research to family–school intervention. *School Psychology Review, 31*(1), 106–121.

Ho Sui-Chu, E., & Willms, J. (1996). Effects of parental involvement on eighth-grade achievement. *Sociology of Education, 69*(2), 126–141.

Lareau, A. (2003). *Unequal childhoods: class, race, and family life.* Berkeley, CA: University of California Press.

Lukes, S. (2003). Promotora training program invests in oral health. *Access, 17*(9), 30–33.

Okpala, C., Okpala, A., & Smith, R. (2001). Parental involvement, instructional expenditures, family socioeconomic attributes, and student achievement. *Journal of Educational Research, 95*(2), 110–115.

Ramos, I., May, M., & Ramos, K. (2001). Environmental health training of promotoras in colonias along the Texas–Mexico border. *American Journal of Public Health, 91,* 568–570.

Snell, P., Miguel, N., & East, J. (2009). Changing directions: Participatory action research as a parent involvement strategy. *Educational Action Research, 17*(2), 239–258.

Sohng, S. (1995). *Participatory research and community organizing.* Paper presented at the New Social Movement and Community Organizing Conference, University of Washington, Seattle.

Trumbull, E., Rothstein-Fisch, C., & Hernandez, E. (2003, Fall/Winter). Parent involvement in schooling: According to whose values? *The School Community Journal, 13*(2), 45–47.

A Response to Chapter 2

Catherine Compton-Lilly

Perhaps the most exciting aspect of the work reported in Chapter 2 is the way the project was initiated. A small group of parents was provided with the methods and materials they needed to work with other parents in their community to address issues related to schooling. This unique organization created forums in which parents could talk, share, and problem-solve. Equally interesting is the fact that this initiative, unlike most family literacy initiatives, which involve the parents of young children, was implemented with middle school parents.

Like the project described in Chapter 1, the project described in this chapter again engages the voices of parents—this time to attend to the obstacles that prevent parents from being involved with their children's schools. Specifically, Snell identifies various situations that complicate school involvement for parents and provides educators with strategies, grounded in the accounts of parents, that encourage parents to become involved. The parents in this study assume leadership roles, demonstrate interest in their children's school learning, and collectively address problems that their children encounter. Participatory action research is a means of engaging parents with schools that recognizes their voices and provides them with opportunities to act in support of their children. We witness parents moving from facing obstacles to parent involvement toward working with schools and teachers.

In the following chapter, Long delves into changes that occurred for parents. She focuses on the ways parents were encouraged to revisit their own school experiences as they took on new academic identities through involvement in a participatory action research community. Through engagement with peers and the support of university facilitators, parents assumed expanded roles as educators and found ways to engage with their children around schooling.

CHAPTER 3

TRANSFORMATIVE CHANGE

Parent Involvement as a Process of Identity Development

Joyce F. Long

During the past 3 years, Stuart Greene and I have interviewed dozens of urban parents in research for the parents' workshop mentioned in Chapter 1. Almost every individual easily answered the question, "As a child, what did you want to be when you grew up?" Collectively, their answers represent a wide variety of careers, including dancers, football players, pediatricians, and lawyers. Their responses indicated that they all had a dream predicated upon acquiring a specific identity. Essentially, their dreams helped shape the person they wanted to become.

A secondary influence on the scope and direction of who we want to become is what we learn; indeed, learning both shapes and is shaped by identity. When children dream of becoming pediatricians, they must successfully learn the content of their biology, chemistry, or anatomy courses in order to achieve that identity. Yet learning, defined as experiences that cause "a relatively permanent change in an individual's knowledge or behavior," can be "deliberate or unintentional, for better or for worse" (Woolfolk, 2005, p. 190), and accurate or incorrect (Hill, 2002). Every academic challenge we successfully overcome reflects our ability to link new information with existing knowledge in meaningful ways (American Psychological Association, 1995), thus securely establishing our identity as learners.

But how are our identities as learners affected when we encounter academic problems that are neither consistently nor successfully resolved? Because forming an identity is neither automatic nor permanently accomplished (Marcia, 1999), students who define themselves as "poor readers" or "lousy in spelling" negatively influence their evolving identity and severely limit what they might accomplish in the future. This is true whether the struggling learners are in high school remedial reading classes, preservice teacher training courses, or parent-involvement workshops. Thus, the purpose of this chapter is to explore how parents may need strategic, interactive opportunities to tear down prior malformed school identities in order to rebuild new self-images that are associated with academic learning, before they can identify themselves as involved parents. Indeed, one recent graduate of NPLB workshops described the program as first helping you to "change yourself" and then to "change what you do."

COMPLICATING COMMONSENSE VIEWS OF URBAN PARENTS' INVOLVEMENT

In a provocatively rich and powerful review of the parent-involvement literature, Pomerantz, Moorman, and Litwack (2007) suggest that future research should direct its attention to interventions that are autonomy-supportive, process-focused, emotionally positive, and associated with constructive beliefs about children's potential. Although some research focuses exclusively upon parent involvement's effect on student achievement (Fan & Chen, 2001), other research highlights the importance of supporting children's autonomy and positive affect as well as healthy identity development (Erikson, 1963).

When parents are given adequate support for effectively navigating through learning crises, they develop autonomy within academic contexts to not only build effective involvement styles, but also reconstruct their own academic identities. In the right environment, parents who previously may have been unsuccessful in specific subjects (e.g., math, reading) can begin to forge new internal descriptions of themselves (e.g., intelligent rather than stupid). Thus parents whose early experiences of formal schooling may have included low-track courses (Oakes, 2005), less interactive pedagogy (Anyon, 1988), seriously diminished motivation levels (Hidi & Harackiewicz, 2000), and savagely high dropout rates (Indiana Department of Education, 2009) may be able to utilize involvement interventions to reformulate their own negative academic self-images acquired through numerous hours and years of failure in school.

APPROACHES TO IDENTITY DEVELOPMENT

Psychological theories of identity development postulate that "internal traits and dispositions" (Smagorinsky, Cook, Moore, Jackson, & Fry, 2004, p. 14) emerge over time as individuals resolve specific conflicts. More specifically, Erikson's (1959) theory of psychosocial development includes eight unique stages: basic trust, autonomy, initiative, industry, identity, intimacy, generativity, and integrity. Within Erikson's model, these concepts are acquired in progressive stages that correspond with chronological ages or grade levels. Although his theory was developed 5 decades ago, its tenets are still emphasized in educational psychology textbooks today. Moreover, it is not unusual for preservice teachers to regularly complete assignments that require applying Erikson's concepts and principles to experiences in their field placements. Thus teachers in training learn that a first-grade student who self-selects a book and loudly expresses the desire to read the book without any help is demonstrating initiative and independence, as well as reading readiness.

Parents likewise might benefit from similar opportunities to successfully solve these same challenges. Whether a person processes them in a linear fashion or concurrently—as described in sociocultural approaches—Erikson (1963) suggests that successfully resolving each crisis heightens one's sense of inner unity, good judgment, and the capacity to succeed in accordance with social and cultural expectations. According to his theory, parents who judge themselves to be trustworthy and capable of accurately assessing another's ability to be trusted have acquired basic trust. In contrast, autonomy emerges in individuals who have experienced environments where independence and rightful dignity are emphasized and shame is minimized during the exercise of free choice. When a third characteristic, initiative, is present in individuals, they can create possibilities, formulate goals, and achieve pleasure through conquests.

Whereas initiative reflects a person's ability to imagine possibilities, industry is formed in individuals as they watch "how things are done" and subsequently try to do them (Erikson, 1959, p. 82). In schools, students can acquire industry whenever they have appropriate opportunities to work and play and learn to be useful. As individuals experience pride in exerting effort, enjoy working, and feel a sense of adequacy rather than inferiority from "doing things beside and with others," they acquire understanding about "division of labor and equality of opportunity" (p. 88). They also become convinced they are "learning effective steps toward a tangible future" (p. 89).

Becoming industrious naturally helps one to define and operate in roles that society and/or culture judges to be meaningful, which in turn builds intimacy by sharing one's likes, dislikes, "plans, wishes, and expectations" (Erikson, 1959, p. 95) with others. Achieving intimacy thus leads to developing a concern for securely guiding and establishing the next generation (generativity) and gaining personal fulfillment through accepting oneself (ego integrity). If identity development does occur in a linear fashion during childhood, trusting kindergarten children who repeatedly experience academic failures by second grade may be stalled and incapable of regarding themselves as industrious academic learners until those processes are successfully renavigated.

Fortunately, sociocultural approaches confirm that identity development can also occur continuously in the midst of contextual interactions (Holland, Lachicotte, Skinner, & Cain, 1998) through "engagement with others in cultural practice" (Smagorinsky et al., 2004, p. 14). This is particularly good news because parents must regard themselves as competent academic learners and informal teachers, if involvement fundamentally includes facilitating student learning at home and in school (Epstein & Van Voorhis, 2001). The literature on teacher identity suggests that ideal environments for identity construction acknowledge the constraints of personal histories and ability beliefs (Olsen, 2008). These environments also provide opportunities for individuals to participate in "new communities of practice" (Freedman & Appleman, 2008, p. 111), which in teacher-training settings include individuals reflectively interacting with the content, their peers, the schools where they work, and new professional networks.

A NOTE ON METHODS

Since our participants and the research setting have already been described thoroughly in Chapter 1, this methods section begins by briefly explaining how the contents of this chapter relate to the larger study and concludes with a more specific focus on how our workshops facilitated identity development. In general, the presurvey and focus group data cited in Chapter 1 informed us that our parents generally did not regard themselves as academic instructors. Instead, they unanimously regarded the schools as doing a good job and viewed their role primarily as getting children to school and monitoring whether homework was completed. Moreover, initial interviews suggested that the majority of parents had not graduated from traditional high school settings. The one participant who attended a 4-year college later dropped out.

In addition to the data sources already mentioned, every parent ($n = 11$) wrote reflections at the end of each workshop. The parents also wrote reports on completing interactive homework assignments with their children. I scrutinized those written documents for factors associated with the literature on both psychosocial and sociocultural approaches to identity development. Another source of contextualized evidence was provided by videotapes at each session; these were triangulated with the written reflective reports and a follow-up focus group transcript to explore identity development over time.

BECOMING ACADEMIC LEARNERS
AND FACILITATORS OF LEARNING

From the onset, the NPLB program intentionally designed a context in which trust, autonomy, and initiative operated in every workshop. Additionally, the university instructors frequently asked parents for their input on nearly every part of the curriculum (e.g., topics, field trip locations, resources). As a result of these proactive efforts, all participants' evaluations of the program referenced feeling accepted, respected, and valued, because, as one parent reported, no one "ever pulled rank with us." Thus parents had the opportunity to develop as learners and informal teachers in a supportive environment throughout the workshops.

Parents as Academic Learners

During our initial interviews with each parent, parents either spoke of liking school or shed tears as they described their school struggles and dashed career dreams. In comparison to those diverse affective experiences, written reflections showed a rich array of positive emotional responses to the curriculum. After reading chapters in a published autobiography of a Black man who had overcome considerable financial and educational handicaps (e.g., single-parent family, low SES, ridiculed by teacher and peers) to become a famous surgeon (Carson, 1990), they wrote of loving the book's contents and really enjoying the read-aloud process. In the second session, after viewing a documentary about the surgeon's life, parents expressed positive regard for the role of reading in the surgeon's development.

Similarly, every parent responded positively to the movie *Akeelah and the Bee* (Burns & Atchison, 2006). Many called the movie "impressive," "touching," or "inspirational." They described themselves as being "sorry" for a boy whose father intensely pressured him, and "sad" as well as "mad" that Akeelah's mother had not been supportive of her desire to participate in the spelling bee. They were also "proud" of Akeelah's spelling ability as it surpassed what most adults could accomplish. One remarked, "I thought the movie would be boring but I enjoyed it. I liked the part that Akeelah reached her dreams even though her father died. She found her talents. I hope that I could find my son's talents."

For some, the curriculum also evoked negative emotions that needed to be resolved. After a session on the role of interests in learning, one mother remarked, "I was saddened because for most of the last 20 years, I've made almost every decision for what was best for someone else—husband, children—so their interests have become mine." Following a discussion about the role emotions play in learning and watching a documentary on Erin Gruwell and her high school students, who cried openly about their experiences in her language arts classroom, parents intensely discussed their experiences with teachers who truly cared and compared them with teachers who did not appear to care.

These examples highlight the growth of parents' positive identities as they successfully navigated through academic content and addressed affective dimensions of their academic identities. We encouraged laughter and fun in our classroom during expressive reading sessions and mathematics games, and provided healthy opportunities to process painful prior school experiences. More specifically, these new successful learning encounters rekindled their desire to be academic learners.

Parents' investments in learning also became visible when they expanded their initial two-sentence reflections into lengthy paragraphs that extended across multiple pages. They often expressed heartfelt appreciation for each evening's events and demonstrated high levels of motivation and engagement. In addition to these affective and motivational findings, parents acquired knowledge and skills in two important areas: subject matter knowledge (e.g., reading/writing) and knowledge about themselves as learners. They learned, for example, the value of observing and creating art, how reading can have more positive outcomes than watching television, and how single mothers can positively influence children's success in school.

They also discovered that "the library has a lot of interesting things to do and read about that [neither] I nor my son knew about," that a "child's emotions can affect schoolwork and learning," and that "corn pops aren't very good nutrition. If they eat it, they also need toast and juice." Similarly, their knowledge about themselves as learners increased exponentially. After visiting the art museum, one parent declared, "Before when I looked at pictures, I never really took the time to really think about the art of it or the artist's reflection." At a superficial level, one could dismiss these simple statements as merely reflecting low-level knowledge acquisition, yet the extent and frequency of such remarks suggested that new identities were being constructed.

All of these comments are consistent with building a sense of efficacy and industry. Parents practiced academic processes in class and through homework assignments that helped them to develop roles valued by our school-oriented society. Moreover, they continually voiced their preferences and developed intimate relations with both parent-peers and instructors. Over time, their emerging identities as successful academic learners became more established and secure, and parents began earnestly and consistently expressing their desire to gain more expertise in helping their children academically.

Parents as Facilitators of Academic Lessons

Throughout the NPLB workshops, parents acquired content and skills. Every time they participated in interactive lessons with their children, such as tasting different foods, cooking, and playing math games, they began developing new identities as facilitators of their child(ren)'s academic learning. After visiting an art museum where they jointly learned how to examine art and make evaluative judgments about the paintings, parents lavished praise on the visit. One parent was pleasurably surprised and enjoyed "talking with [my son] about the picture he was looking at and helping him see more than just the picture." Another "thought it was an exciting trip because my kids and I have never been to a museum before. They thought it was great." These remarks indicated how much parents appreciated interacting with their children in settings that promoted learning.

Parents experienced this same pride and emotional satisfaction during literacy lessons. In one workshop, the instructors focused on identifying one-, two-, and three-syllable words as well as antonyms/synonyms in the dictionary. We began the lesson by modeling the process of identifying and recording our responses on an accompanying sheet. Then we encouraged the parents to complete each step of the process independently; finally, we observed them practicing with a parent-partner prior to leading their children through the same procedures later in the evening. In this manner, parents had ample opportunities to comfortably learn tasks with supportive, noncritical guidance before they assumed responsibility for instructing their children. Our classroom environment provided multiple opportunities to experience positive emotion, effortful labor, and enhanced understanding as they negotiated stages in building academic identity.

Parents also learned to navigate instructional challenges by applying a three-part strategy to their children's lessons and homework assignments: observe, discuss, and do. One mother helped her second grader learn spelling words. First, she directed her son to visually examine the words, then they discussed the meaning of each word together, and finally she asked him to write the words independently. Another parent designed a lesson for learning fractions, and a third family used these steps to read books. Together they looked at all the pictures, then discussed possible storylines based on the pictures, and finally the child read the book aloud while comparing the hypothesized storyline with the actual text.

Parents also extended their instructional influence to other children in their family. They even practiced newly acquired skills with preschoolers and children above 4th grade. Some created spelling lessons for the entire family from words used in their day-to-day conversations. Others used a phonics text with all family members, inspiring older children to help their younger siblings. In this way, they were securely guiding and establishing literate patterns for the next generation.

Parents' growing competence and confidence in reinforcing and building their children's literacy and numeracy skills began influencing other actions. For example, one mother described previously throwing away all of her children's papers from their backpacks—regardless of the grades they earned. After attending our workshops, she proudly displayed their papers on her refrigerator and encouraged them to work harder by competing for weekly prizes that she awarded for the highest grade. Although she had not received instruction on those specific strategies, her actions reflected dispositional improvement that positively supported her children's academic outcomes.

Examples of changed perception and action related to children's learning also emerged in other, nonacademic areas. For example, after learning about nutrition, sampling healthier foods, and cooking with their children, parents began buying whole grain products and fresh fruits/vegetables, and gave their children toast and juice for breakfast instead of sugar-rich treats. They soon concluded that cooking together builds "independence and measurement skills," even as it "helps with math, reading, teamwork, following directions, and social skills," and building "self-esteem and confidence." Moreover, they consistently demonstrated to their children that learning could be "fun" and could bring families "closer together."

These actions confirmed to both parents and children that they reaped benefits from practicing academic skills together (e.g., phonics, math, reading). Over time, parents described their children as making progress. For instance, a 3rd grader no longer needed his mother's help because "he understands what he's doing." Another parent became more aware of her child's academic challenges: "The first time we did the drill book, I must admit, I was scared and concerned. My son only scored a 55 and stumbled over four of the words. [It was an] eye opener!" After reaching these conclusions, many parents independently crafted instructional goals: "in order for me to keep it up, I am going to keep working with him, and not let him watch so much television." Another optimistically suggested, "We'll keep working over the summer and hopefully by next year, she'll be doing a lot better."

Their instructional plans often included accessing existing community resources, especially the public library. After visiting the public library as a field trip (e.g., attending story hour, taking a tour, finding books related to personal interests), parents were enthusiastic. "We really enjoyed the trip because it gave us time together . . . and it has gotten my son a lot more interested in reading. I am very proud of him in that aspect." One parent attentively noted that her son "likes the children's section of the library. First he played on the computer; then he looked around for a couple of books. He picked out two that he liked and we checked them out. He likes many types of books." Another remarked, "As we toured the grounds from top to bottom, an idea came into my head that this is a great place to have a summer activity at least once a week." They concluded that visiting the library more often would expose their children to "a lot more things."

Over time, they redefined their initial descriptions of teachers being solely responsible for children's academic learning. They began portraying themselves in roles that involved more than correcting behavior. At the last workshop, they listed the following activities to illustrate the many changes they had implemented through their participation in the program: limiting children's television and computer use, requiring children to read two books per week, discussing topics of interest with their children, listening to them read, taking more time with them, feeding them healthier foods, working together, checking homework more thoroughly, working equally hard with all their children, and devoting time to other activities besides school. As they learned from their own mastery experiences and vicariously acquired knowledge from their peers and workshop leaders, they even began questioning their children's principals and teachers in meaningful ways: "Where are the directions on these homework pages?" "How can our children be doing so poorly on standardized test scores but getting As and Bs on their report cards?"

In sum, parents acquired roles as academic learners and informal academic instructors. Three months later at a follow-up focus group, the extent of their growth was still evident when one mother of a single-parent household presented a problem she was having with her son and asked for help. Immediately, the room was charged with passionate remarks from other parents at the table. They encouraged her to take responsibility: "He's your child and he needs you." They also suggested that she start "taking him to church." This exchange not only contrasted strongly with their previous isolation, but indicated they had become more secure in their own identities and could intimately share expertise with others in a like-minded supportive community of practice (Freedman & Appleman, 2008).

These outcomes are especially important for two reasons: First, members of some segments of society have tended erroneously to classify poor individuals with a history of academic struggles as beyond hope and resistant to change (Kozol, 2005); and second, schools that are failing to single-handedly produce verifiable levels of academic improvement desperately need parents who believe they can help their children learn academic skills and content. When parents are empowered to reforge new academic identities, they have an opportunity to intervene on their children's behalf before unhealthy identities take hold.

POSSIBILITIES FOR YOUR CLASSROOM, SCHOOL, AND COMMUNITY

Unfortunately, school administrators tend to narrowly define parent involvement as mimicking the role of teachers (e.g., monitoring the completion of curricular sheets done in school). To singularly limit parents' roles to school-like activities such as getting children to school and completing homework is myopic. A more enlightened approach empowers parents to extend existing lessons and freely construct lessons that enrich formal schooling. Helping parents redefine their academic roles *can* be accomplished. But it requires schools to offer concrete learning experiences that facilitate the attainment of successful outcomes for parents.

The following suggestions are practical ways to begin to support this process. As a classroom teacher, it is important to ask parents whether the directions on homework sheets are clear. Sometimes textbook publishers' instructions are unintelligible to parents who are unfamiliar with content knowledge. Instructions should incorporate language that even a novice reader can interpret correctly. In addition, parents appreciate having access to the standards teachers cover as well as supplemental suggestions for simple home activities or free community field trips that reinforce corresponding requisite skills/content.

We also suggest that schools regularly offer workshops for parents in every core subject. These workshops should provide opportunities for parents to collaborate with one another and practice skills that they can teach their children.

Finally, school administrators can hire parents as part-time helpers in classrooms. A similar program currently is operating in our city, and preliminary results indicate that parents appreciate actually witnessing what teachers do, so that they understand the purpose behind specific homework assignments and pedagogical practices. Moreover, as teachers and parents spend more time together, they develop mutual respect for their respective skills and expertise. In the end, it is imperative that we stop undermining and devaluing this unique role of urban parents, and begin investing resources into reformulating their academic identities as competent learners and informal instructors.

REFERENCES

American Psychological Association. (1995). *Learner-centered psychological principles: A framework for school redesign and reform.* Washington, DC: Author.

Anyon, J. (1988). Social class and the hidden curriculum of work. In G. Handel (Ed.), *Childhood socialization* (pp. 357–382). Hawthorne, NY: Aldine de Gruyter.

Burns, M. (Producer), & Atchison, D. (Writer/Director). (2006). *Akeelah and the bee* [Motion picture]. Santa Monica, CA: Lions Gate Films.

Carson, B. (1990). *Gifted hands.* Grand Rapids, MI: Zondervan.

Epstein, J. L., & Van Voorhis, F. L. (2001). More than minutes: Teachers' roles in designing homework. *Educational Psychologist, 36,* 181–193.

Erikson, E. H. (1959). *Identity and the life cycle.* New York: International Universities Press.

Erikson, E. H. (1963). *Childhood and society* (2nd ed.). New York: Norton.

Fan, X., & Chen, M. (2001). Parental involvement and students' academic achievement: A meta-analysis. *Educational Psychology Review, 13,* 1–22.

Freedman, S. W., & Appleman, D. (2008). "What else would I be doing?": Teacher identity and teacher retention in urban schools. *Teacher Education Quarterly, 35*(3), 109–126.

Hidi, S., & Harackiewicz, J. M. (2000). Motivating the academically unmotivated: A critical issue for the 21st century. Review of Educational Research, 70(2), 151–180.

Hill, W. F. (2002). *Learning: A survey of psychological interpretations* (7th ed.). Boston: Allyn & Bacon.

Holland, D., Lachicotte, W., Skinner, D., & Cain, C. (1998). *Identity and agency in cultural worlds.* Cambridge, MA: Harvard University Press.

Indiana Department of Education. (2009). *2008 local school corporation graduation rates* [Data file]. Available at http://www.doe.in.gov/data/

Kozol, J. (2005). *The shame of the nation.* New York: Crown.

Marcia, J. E. (1999). Representational thought in ego identity, psychotherapy, and psychosocial developmental theory. In I. E. Sigel (Ed.), *Development of mental representation: Theories and application* (pp. 391–414). Mahwah, NJ: Erlbaum.

Oakes, J. (2005). *Keeping track* (2nd ed.). New Haven, CT: Yale University Press.

Olsen, B. (2008). How reasons for entry into the profession illuminate teacher identity development. *Teacher Education Quarterly, 35*(3), 23–40.

Pomerantz, E. M., Moorman, E. A., & Litwack, S. D. (2007). The how, whom, and why of parent involvement in children's academic lives: More is not always better. *Review of Educational Research, 77*(3), 373–410.

Smagorinsky, P., Cook, L. S., Moore, C., Jackson, A. Y., & Fry, P. G. (2004). Tensions in learning to teach: Accommodation and the development of a teacher identity. *Journal of Teacher Education, 55*(1), 8–24.

Woolfolk, A. (2005). *Educational psychology* (9th ed.). Boston: Allyn & Bacon.

A Response to Chapter 3

Catherine Compton-Lilly

Chapter 3, Long draws on the same study reported on in Chapter 1 and focuses on the academic identities of parents and the role they play as informal educators in their children's lives. In doing so, she challenges the assumption that some parents are less prepared than others to support their children in school. As parents told stories of themselves as academic learners, viewed films depicting the academic stories of others, and participated in a series of workshops designed to meet their interests as learners, they reflected on memorable and problematic learning experiences in their own lives and made decisions about how they wanted to work with their own children. Collectively they designed learning experiences for their children and shared the learning practices that occurred in their own homes—each parent drawing on the experiences and knowledge of the others.

Long reminds us that celebrating the differences that children bring to school is essential but not enough. We also need to support parents who choose to redefine themselves as agents capable of helping their children. As Long explains, "It is imperative that we stop undermining and devaluing the unique role of urban parents, and begin investing resources into reformulating their academic identities as competent learners and informal instructors."

Long's chapter highlights the academic abilities of parents and invites them to act as agents in their own children's learning. The final chapter in Part I also addresses the agency of parents, this time as community activists working for the welfare of children.

CHAPTER 4

PARENT INVOLVEMENT
WITH A **PURPOSE**

Get the Lead Out!

Rebecca Rogers
Darren O'Brien

Some parents in St. Louis are angry that 27 grade schools have potential lead paint hazards, but the district does not have the money to fix the problem. . . . "I think it's just unconscionable that some solution can't be found," said Darren O'Brien, the father of two grade school children.

(12/2/08, Associated Press)

On a cold morning in December 2008, several dozen people attended a rally outside Roe Elementary School in St. Louis to demand that the district remove lead hazards from the school buildings. A press release was circulated days before reminding people of the dangers of lead in the city's public schools and asking them to attend the rally to publicly insist on the lead removal. The State Appointed Board (SAB) had moved the Wilkinson Early Childhood Center to Roe School, even though it was so lead contaminated that the YMCA had to forego before- and after-school care for children under 6. It was here that I (Rebecca) would see Darren O'Brien's parent involvement in action.

I walked to the rally to support parent-led community activism at my local school. I deeply believe that the kinds of complex, daily literacy practices that families use to accomplish important social goals can serve as inspiration for designing educational reforms. As I joined the crowd on the school's steps, I realized that Darren O'Brien's advocacy was one such case.

Darren is a White man and father of two children in the school district and vice-president of the PTO and chair of its advocacy committee. As part of his speech to the crowd of supporters and the media, Darren stated:

Children that are coming from a home where there is a lead hazard, and then come to a school that has the same hazard, are in double jeopardy. Shouldn't a school be a refuge from that type of danger? Until local, state, and federal agencies can sufficiently address the residential danger, shouldn't the schools at least be a safe haven?

The school district, mired in political and economic turmoil, recently had been taken over by the state and was now run not by an elected school board but by a State Appointed Board (Downs, n.d., Portz, Stein, & Jones, 1999; Rogers & Pole, 2009). While the elected school board made room in the budget to abate the lead in schools over a 5-year period, the SAB removed the money for the lead abatement from the budget. They then reported that there was no money for lead abatement. At the same time, the SAB was paying a management company half a million dollars to assess the facilities in the district and make recommendations about school closings. Ironically, in their final report, the company would not report on the high lead levels in 28 of the district schools, a finding demonstrated in earlier reports.

COMPLICATING COMMONSENSE VIEWS OF
LITERACY, FAMILY, AND COMMUNITY

Darren's talk at this rally reflected years of groundwork (50 years in St. Louis) laid by other parents, politicians, and community members about the hazards of lead contaminants for children in homes and schools in St. Louis. This rally (and Associated Press coverage) set in motion a series of events that ultimately resulted in the CEO of the district publicly stating that the district would look for resources to abate the lead from all school buildings. Over the next several months, Darren's and my paths crossed several times at events, meetings, and demonstrations where we joined others in advocating for the health and education of students and families in the St. Louis public schools (SLPS).

In this chapter, co-authored by a researcher and a parent, we share the series of events that led to the district committing funds to begin lead abatement in the schools. We offer this narrative of family literacy and parent involvement from the perspectives of a parent and a researcher/ recently elected board member—both citizens concerned with the health and vitality of the SLPS.

LEAD POISONING AS ENVIRONMENTAL RACISM

The effects of environmental hazards such as lead disproportionately impact people of color, the poor, and the working class. Guinier and Torres (2002) define racism as "acquiescence in and accommodation to racialized hierarchies governing resource distribution, generation and transfer of resources as normal, natural, and fair" (p. 292).

By and large the impacts of lead hazards have been overlooked and action has been neglected because it was perceived that the communities affected most by lead were politically powerless. It was assumed they would not protest such environmental hazards for fear of losing homes or employment. The metaphor of the miner's canary highlights the racism in how environmental issues such as lead poisoning in homes and schools are addressed. As Guinier and Torres (2002) explain, we wait until the canary dies to respond to known hazards. Dr. Barry Commoner, Director for the Center for Biology of Natural Systems at Washington University, in 1971 warned St. Louis against the dangers of using children as lead detectors. He stated:

> The way we know an apartment has lead on the walls is that a child gets sick. It's exactly the way a miner uses a canary in the mine. If a canary keels over, then he knows he's in trouble. But we're using children as canaries. (Commoner, 1971, cited in St. Louis Lead Prevention Coalition, 2003, p. 3)

Racism is a condition that pathologizes the canary, explaining the canary's condition, in this case lead poisoning, as its own problem. Without further examination of the structural conditions of the mines, or schools, a dominant cultural narrative blames depressed socioeconomic, health, and educational experiences on those who experience oppression. This narrative depends on those with privileged access to resources (e.g., sending their children to private or county schools) being complacent in the unfair distribution of lead-free public schools.

As Moore (2003) points out, there is a mounting body of evidence that demonstrates how environmental racism puts an immeasurable burden on the education of America's children. Children exposed to pollutants such as lead or asbestos are impacted in areas of memory, learning, attention, motor skills, personality, and emotions. Children are exposed to lead in many ways: through air, drinking water, food, contaminated soil, deteriorating paint, and dust.

In St. Louis, children are poisoned by lead at nearly six times the national average (Higgins, 2000). In 2000, 31% of the tested children under age 6 in St. Louis suffered from lead poisoning; the highest rates clustered in the African American community.

Lead has been a recognized concern, resulting in the deaths of children in St. Louis since at least 1946, and lead abatement has been used as a political platform for more than 6 decades (Lipsitz, 2006). Yet, despite mayoral promises, insufficient funding coupled with inappropriate uses of funds have resulted in a relative standstill around the removal of lead hazards from homes and schools, and the focus has been on secondary prevention rather than eliminating the conditions that cause lead poisoning (Fitz, 2006).

St. Louis Lead Prevention Coalition, started in 2001, consists of representatives of the city, the school, health clinicians, and families with lead-poisoned children. Together with the Health and Environmental Justice and the Gateway Green Alliance, they rallied to draw attention to the city's inadequate lead programs and policies that required parents to prove that their child had been poisoned by lead in order to receive support for lead abatement.

But progress has been even slower in responding to lead hazards in schools where children spend 6 to 8 hours of each day. Over the past 8 years, the revolving door of the superintendency in the district has ushered in varying degrees of commitment to lead abatement. Lead abatement has become a political-race project among the superintendents and the politicians in the city, each one addressing it rhetorically but not materially. Indeed, the history of St. Louis's efforts of lead removal is characterized by a refusal to "enforce its own laws and to allocate sufficient funds to detoxify the bloodstreams of children and to remove lead hazards from their homes, playgrounds and schools" (Lipsitz, 2006, p. 3).

Our approach to parent involvement recognizes race, class, and gender—frameworks often invisible in discussions of parent involvement (for exceptions, see Compton-Lilly, 2003; Greene & Abt-Perkins, 2003; Rogers, 2003; Whitehouse & Colvin, 2001). We also draw on what Auerbach (1989) refers to as an "empowerment" approach in which parents use language and literacy to advocate for better educational circumstances for their children. In this paradigm, parent involvement is used not to reinforce schooled practices but to *change* schooled practices. Parents are positioned as agents of social change, whose resources can be used to restructure schools (Delgado-Gaitan, 1991, 2001; Osterling, 2001).

A NOTE ON METHODS

We intend for this narrative to be read as an example of "engaged scholarship." Engaged scholarship is situated within a tradition of dialogic, emancipatory education (Collins, 2000; Freire, 1970). Our observations, experiences, and dialogues move us to deeper understandings of social conditions. As Darren and I learned more about issues related to lead poisoning, we were in better positions to act. This engagement with the social world was at the core of our methodology—a process of "researching social change and changing the researcher" (Delgado-Gaitan, 1993, p. 389).

Procedurally, Darren and I recreated his experiences of working on getting the lead out of schools. His narrative provided the core of our analysis. Next, we situated his narrative within a larger sociohistorical context of lead abatement efforts in St. Louis. From here, we traced learning about lead contaminants, educating other parents about the issues, and advocating for the removal of lead in all schools. We traced the range of literacy practices that Darren used in his advocacy work—community newsletters, speeches, panel presentations, media, and leaflets. It is these textual practices that formed the basis of our analysis. As we wrote this chapter, we both continued to learn more about the hazards of lead as a nationwide problem as well as efforts to remedy the problem.

STOP USING CHILDREN AS LEAD DETECTORS: GET THE LEAD OUT!

While committed to sending his children to public schools, Darren did not consider himself to be an "activist type." However, what was personal, the health of his children, became political—fighting the school district for lead removal. Darren was moved to action: "I had never been inclined toward activism before 2004, but from the first year my daughter started school, there has been one issue after another which risked undermining the well-being of our school and district." Darren came to the realization that many of the problems in the district were a result of politics, not about reforming educational conditions for children. He recalled:

> I reached a point where I decided that I could not stand idly by
> and watch. I felt that I had to get involved for the sake of my chil-
> dren and the other children of the district. Even while involved,
> I never held out much hope. . . . But the efforts of the parents at
> my children's school and the events that those efforts set in mo-
> tion, have changed my impression . . . advocacy can make a dif-
> ference.

Darren recognized the dangers of environmental toxins to his children as well as environmental racism that had consequences for everyone. As Guinier and Torres (2002) wrote, "The content and experience of racism varies depending on the local conditions, but like the air we breathe or the economic system we share, it affects us all" (p. 292). Darren worked to disrupt these racial hierarchies by changing the face of those connected with lead poisoning.

Parents Educating Parents

Darren and his wife moved to St. Louis in 2000. As they assimilated to life in the city, they learned more about the hazards of lead in city homes and schools. During this time, the City Health Department sent out notices, warning parents of lead hazards. Fliers with the following information appeared in their mailbox:

What you don't know about lead poisoning can hurt your child.
Learn more about lead paint and other hazards.
Call 1-800-424-LEAD
Let's give every child a lead-safe home

Their reading of this literature, alongside discussions with other parents, raised a growing concern: Were their children safe from lead poisoning?

As Darren recalled, yellow-tape fences around the houses that were being abated were a routine sight during the early 2000s, as families throughout the city became aware of the hazards of lead poisoning. Around the same time, the Parents as Teachers program was educating parents about lead hazards and offered free screenings for parents, which Darren and his wife took advantage of for their daughter Hannah (age 3 at the time). Hannah, luckily, did not have high levels from her home environment.

However, for those families who were not so lucky, parents had to both prove that their child had been poisoned by lead and provide the money upfront for the lead abatement, in order to apply for the city tax credits for lead abatement in homes. Thus, only families with financial means received the help desperately needed by so many in the community.

In Fall 2004, Darren's 4½-year-old daughter started prekindergarten at Kennard Classical Junior Academy. The next year, the program was moved to Roe Elementary, a staging school, for 1 year while Kennard was renovated to add air conditioning. Darren and other parents in the school hoped that the school's lead hazards would be addressed at the same time. However, not only were the hazards ignored, but parents later learned that the Roe staging school that students had been moved to also had a lead hazard. Eventually, the fences around the perimeter of Kennard were painted to encapsulate the lead, but that was the extent of lead abatement.

In 2007, Darren's son started pre-K at Wilkinson Early Childhood Center (a program for children ages 3½ through grade 2). Parents supported the early childhood program and liked the building, which was designed for young children. During the summer of 2008, the SAB moved this early childhood center to Roe, the same school that had served as a staging site for his daughter's school. This decision was made despite earlier reports of high lead levels.

Not surprisingly, the parents were confused and angered by this move. At the beginning of the school year, health hazards became apparent to parents when the YMCA discontinued its before- and after-school care programs for children under age 6 due to code violations related to lead paint and fire inspections.

These and other experiences catapulted Darren into becoming active with the PTOs at his children's schools, investing in the activism that had been kindled when he first had his daughter tested for lead poisoning. He joined the board as the district liaison officer and attended district meetings, school board meetings, and parent assembly meetings. The following year, he was elected vice-president of the PTO and chair of its advocacy committee, which decided to make lead hazards at school the focus of their advocacy efforts.

Going Public with Information

The information from the school building reports coupled with the general instability of the district laid the backdrop for growing parent unrest. The efforts of the parent groups coalesced to a point where Darren found himself in the middle of efforts to force the district to deal with the lead issue in the schools. During this phase, Darren used many different kinds of literacy practices—speeches, reports, presentations, and emails—to educate others (including myself) about the hazards of lead poisoning in the district's schools. Darren noted how the parents worked together and took on various roles throughout the campaign. A parent who was a nurse initiated reading and interpreting the lead levels for each of the buildings. Another parent, a lawyer, became a strong advocate around legal matters. Another mother wrote a presentation that was made to the SAB. Other parents emailed questions to district officials, requested information, collected historical information, and presented at meetings. Darren organized an email group to enable parents to stay connected. Parents used a range of tools to insist that schools be made lead free.

Darren joined with other parents in October 2008 to address the State Appointed Board in a public meeting:

> We never thought in 2008 we would have to be concerned about lead paint in an early childhood center. This is serious health concern for over 200 3- to 8-year-olds. . . . We are concerned regarding a statement that the operations manager made in which he stated that most of the public school buildings have lead paint on the exterior—windows, soffits, doors. . . . The exterior paint on the windows at Roe is in poor repair to the visible eye.

Despite the fact that the "healthy seats" report showed high levels of lead in 28 elementary schools, the SAB again removed money for abatement from the district budget. Parent grassroots organizations responded.

Several months later, in the midst of an ongoing mayoral campaign, the Gateway Green Alliance, an organization with a long history of advocating for lead-free homes and schools (e.g., Fitz, 2006), organized a rally in front of Roe Elementary to highlight the lead hazards in the district's schools. Darren O'Brien was the main speaker. Standing in the cold with two dozen other people, Darren spoke:

> No amount of lead exposure is safe. While 2- and 3-year-old children are most at risk, all of the children here are at some level of risk. . . . Of the 28 schools on the district's list for needing remediation/abatement, 26 of them have pre-k level classes, among some of them are 3-year-olds. . . . Along with all of the other safety issues that any public school building needs to address, lead remediation/abatement should be one of them. It is unacceptable that the school district does not have a plan already in place to remove or remedy the lead hazard here.

The Associated Press covered the rally, and the story was disseminated by nearly every media outlet in the city. Later, Darren and I reflected on the coverage of the rally. While Darren believed that the Associated Press report was well done, other stories included only bits of information. Darren recognized the potential of alternative media forms to inform the public and put pressure on the district. He shared his concerns through newsletters, panel presentations, and public access TV. Darren and I were both asked to be panelists for a forum in February 2008 called "Rebuilding St. Louis Public Schools" organized by the Gateway Green Alliance. At the forum, Darren claimed a position of authority as a parent. As a White male, people listened to him. Darren was asked, If "you know the schools have lead in them, why do you leave your children in those schools?" by an African American man in the audience. This question implied that

Darren had a choice and the privilege to move his children out of the city schools. Darren chose to use his privilege to advocate for lead-free schools for all children.

Around this same time, the local teachers' union joined the advocacy efforts to address lead in schools. Under the Missouri Sunshine Law, Chapter 610, it requested "all lead and asbestos testing reports for the SLPS from 1999 to the present," and criticized the lack of full disclosure of hazardous materials in the comprehensive report of facilities, and the district's painfully slow process for addressing the lead toxins in schools.

The Promise of Lead Removal

Not long after the rally and the resulting media attention, the CEO of the SAB announced that the board would reverse its stance on lead and seek outside sources of funding to deal with the problem (during the summer of 2008, the SAB had again removed lead abatement money from its budget).

The SAB applied for stimulus money to cover the lead abatement of schools. In June 2009, the SAB approved a $9.4 million contract for total lead abatement at 25 elementary schools, including window replacement. However, several weeks later the contract was reduced to $2.4 million and focused only on hazardous materials, due to the high costs of window replacement.

Principles of environmental justice must be read within a racial framework in which White people hold at least equal, if not more, responsibility for change. Guiner and Torres (2002) explain:

> Even though the canary is in a cage, it continues to have agency and voice. If the miners were watching the canary, they would not wait for it to fall off its perch, legs up. They would notice that it is talking to them. "I can't breathe, but you know what? You are being poisoned, too. If you save me, you will save yourself." The miners might then realize that they cannot escape this life-threatening social arrangement without a strategy that disrupts the way things are. (p. 261)

POSSIBILITIES FOR YOUR CLASSROOM, SCHOOL, AND COMMUNITY

The case of parent involvement around removing lead hazards that we have shared in this chapter is, in some ways, ordinary. It is the kind of work that parents carry out when their children attend urban schools around the nation. Yet it is a story that deserves documenting, analyzing, sharing, and reflecting on. For purposes of this chapter, the history of lead poisoning and advocacy for lead removal in St. Louis has been shortened, but it is reported on elsewhere (e.g., Fitz, 2006; Lipsitz, 1989). We believe that this narrative of parents working together provides a powerful example for others who are interested in the social welfare of children in schools. We believe that this case adds to the field of parent involvement in three ways.

First, parent involvement and family literacy historically have been considered women's work (Luttrell, 1996; Pitt, 2008). Darren's case is a mix of traditionally sanctioned parent involvement (e.g., attending meetings) and less traditional involvement using a wide range of literacy practices to advocate for better educational conditions. We need to stress that it is not just parent involvement that is so desperately needed in our schools but the *types* of parent involvement that have real purposes and real effects for children. Naples (1998) refers to the type of involvement that leads to changes in social conditions as "activist mothering." Based on this case, we would extend this construct to "activist parenting." We believe that it is the kind of advocacy work that is an important example of the power of men and women working together to make public education stronger.

Second, the chapter brings together parent involvement and new literacy studies. In this chapter we have shared the literacy practices that Darren used to advocate for better educational conditions. It is this process and the product of these literacy practices—speeches, forming online networking sites, collecting reports, organizing parents, speaking at board meetings, using alternative forms of media—that result in better health and educational conditions for children. Why wouldn't we recognize, encourage, and build on these social practices? When we see the vast potential that parents have when they work together on behalf of their children, why would we limit parent involvement to test preparation, chaperoning homework, and assisting in classrooms?

Parent involvement is undoubtedly is a key element in educational reform. How we understand parent involvement, though—as narrowly defined by the school or more expansively defined as engagement with public policy issues that impact children—impacts what we ask for, expect from, and envision for parents. The parent involvement of a small group of dedicated parents led the school district closer to abating the lead from 25 elementary schools. Their involvement had a catalytic impact on the district and on other citizens, including myself. As a citizen, the parents educated me about the history and politics of lead in St. Louis. As an elected board member, I wrote a resolution in support of the lead abatement initiative in the schools.

Parent involvement is a part of civic engagement and, in that sense, is intricately tied not only to the health of our nation's schools but also to the health of our democracy. Dewey (1907) stated:

> What the best and wisest parent wants for his own child, that must the community want for all of its children. Any other ideal for our schools is narrow and unlovely; acted upon, it destroys our democracy. (p. 34)

The existence of lead in schools destroys the public space of schools. It raises the social costs of educating children who have been poisoned by lead (e.g., environmental racism, continued stratification of society through tracking, shrinking public spaces). It makes us all less healthy. The social responsibility for lead-free homes and schools should fall under the responsibility of the public domain. However, history has proven otherwise. Only through the efforts of parents and citizens can pressure be put on elected officials to make the city lead free. Parents committed to the promises of public education recognize that the interests of their child and all children are reciprocal. Thus, when parents advocate—using language and literacy practices—for better educational conditions for their child, they also are advocating for better conditions for all children.

The third contribution of our work is the deliberate placement of parent involvement within a racial-political framework. Within this framework, the literacy practices that exist within Darren's home around lead hazards are, themselves, racialized. The same paperwork (i.e., notices about testing your children for lead poisoning) would not be found in the home of a family living in the suburbs of St. Louis. Further, Darren's involvement as a parent around lead hazards needs also to be read within a racial framework. How might his involvement as a White man been read differently from that of a White mother or a Black father? As we have argued, while the lead issues disproportionately impact children of color, the social costs impact everyone in society. I am reminded of the question asked of Darren during the panel forum: "Why do you leave your children in those schools?" Darren's commitment to public education exposes the moral peril of the lead issue and for all children. Darren's advocacy makes the congruence of interests between Black, Brown, and White communities more obvious.

While there have been some teacher-led initiatives around the hazards of lead poisoning from schools around the country (Compton-Lilly, 2004; Dawson Salas, 2003; Ness, 2003), fewer reports have advocated or supported parents in fighting for lead-free schools, an absence we address in our chapter. Thus, we can see in Darren's case a story of how parent involvement led toward getting the lead cleaned out of schools, but we also can hear a parallel story of how his commitment led to his increased efficacy as a parent. His involvement as a parent serves as a reminder of the power of public education as a public space.

REFERENCES

Auerbach, E. R. (1989). Toward a socio-contextual approach to family literacy. *Harvard Educational Review, 59,* 165–181.

Collins, P. (2000). *Black feminist thought: Knowledge, consciousness, and the politics of empowerment.* New York: Routledge.

Compton-Lilly, C. (2003). *Reading families: The literate lives of urban children.* New York: Teachers College Press.

Compton-Lilly, C. (2004). A school-wide project: Learning about lead poisoning. In C. Compton-Lilly (Ed.), *Confronting racism, poverty and power: Classroom strategies to change the world* (pp. 97–104). Portsmouth, NH: Heinemann.

Dawson Salas, K. (2003). Teaching about toxins. *Rethinking Schools, 18*(2). Retrieved May 14, 2009, from http://www.rethinkingschools.org/archive/18_02/toxi182/shtml

Delgado-Gaitan, C. (1991). Involving parents in the schools: A process of empowerment. *American Journal of Education, 11,* 20–26.

Delgado-Gaitan, C. (1993). Researching change and changing the researcher. *Harvard Educational Review, 63*(4), 389–411.

Delgado-Gaitan, C. (2001). *The power of community: Mobilizing for family and schooling.* New York: Rowman & Littlefield.

Dewey, J. (1907). *Schools and society.* Boston: Educational Publishing Company.

Downs, P. (n.d.). *This is reform? The plot to kill public education in an American city and the struggle to stop it.* Unpublished manuscript.

Fitz, D. (2006). Lead follies in St. Louis. *Synthesis/Regeneration, 41.* Retrieved May 10, 2009, from http://www.greens.org/s-r/41/41-07.html

Freire, P. (1970). *Pedagogy of the oppressed.* New York: Continuum.

Greene, S., & Abt-Perkins, D. (2003). *Making race visible: Literacy research for cultural understanding.* New York: Teachers College Press.

Guinier, L., & Torres, G. (2002). *The miner's canary: Enlisting race, resisting power, transforming democracy.* Cambridge, MA: Harvard University Press.

Higgins, L. (2000). The lead menace. *The Riverfront Times.* Retrieved February, 10, 2009, from http://www.riverfronttimes.com/2000-04-12/news/the-lead-menace/

Lipsitz, G. (1989). *A life in the struggle: Ivory Perry and the culture of opposition.* Philadelphia: Temple University Press.

Lipsitz, G. (2006). Ivory Perry and the fight against lead poisoning in St. Louis. *Synthesis/Regeneration, 41,* 1–4. Retrieved May 11, 2009, from http://www.greens.org/s-r/41/41-06.html

Luttrell, W. (1996). Taking care of literacy: One feminist's critique. *Educational Policy, 19*(3), 342–365.

Moore, C. (2003). *Silent scourge: Children, pollution and why scientists disagree*. Oxford: Oxford University Press.

Naples, N. (1998). *Grassroots warriors: Activist mothers, community work and the war on poverty*. New York: Routledge.

Ness, E. (2003, Winter). Getting the lead out. *Rethinking Schools, 18*(2) 18–21.

Osterling, J. P. (2001). Waking the sleeping giant: Engaging and capitalizing on the socio-cultural strengths of the Latino community. *Bilingual Research Journal, 25*, 59–88.

Pitt, K. (2008). Being a new capitalist mother. In M. Pinsloo & M. Baynham (Eds.), *Literacies, global and local* (pp. 51–70). Amsterdam: John Benjamins.

Portz, J., Stein, L., & Jones, R. (1999). *City schools, city politics: Institutions and leadership in Pittsburgh, Boston, and St. Louis*. Kansas City: University of Kansas Press.

Rogers, R. (2003). *A critical discourse analysis of family literacy practices: Power in and out of print*. Mahwah, NJ: Erlbaum.

Rogers, R., & Pole, K. (2009). A state takeover: The language of a school district crisis. In L. MacGillivray (Ed.), *Literacy practices in times of crisis* (pp. 138–158). New York: Routledge.

St. Louis Lead Prevention Coalition. (2003). *Lead canaries: The tragic tradition of childhood lead poisoning in St. Louis*. [report] Retrieved May 10, 2009, from http://www.leadprevention.org/scripts/report.cfm

Whitehouse, M., & Colvin, C. (2001). Reading families: Deficit discourses and family literacy. *Theory Into Practice, 40*(3), 212–219.

A Response to Chapter 4

Catherine Compton-Lilly

In Chapter 4, Rogers and O'Brien take up the theme of agency in a new way. They report on a shared journey that led to a school district committing funds to lead abatement in the schools. Theirs is a story of both parent involvement and family literacy as they describe the ways O'Brien and other parents drew upon their literacy practices to lobby for change in their community.

Rogers and O'Brien draw specific attention to the ways in which policies related to economics, health service, and schooling intersect with race and social class. Lead poisoning is a problem that disproportionately affects poor and racially diverse communities. Rather than fleeing these communities and their schools, White parents and scholars can use their unearned privilege in the service of communities of color to address inequities and advocate for all children. In addition to calling attention to race and social class, the authors challenge traditional models of gender and parenting—depicting a father, rather than the traditional mother, as being deeply involved in schooling and working on the behalf of children.

Rogers and O'Brien's work demonstrates the importance and power of calling upon existing networks, including PTOs, advocacy meetings, and opportunities to present at public meetings such as school board meetings. This chapter reveals the power of parent and researcher working together and how this model of parent involvement can lead not only to social change but also to increased efficacy as parents recognize the power they have to effect needed change.

Across the chapters in Part I, the authors challenge traditional definitions of parent involvement and advocate for new forms of parent participation. Participatory action research, community-based research initiatives, parents as informal educators, and parents as activists are all presented as possibilities that can re-imagine and redefine the roles parents play in children's school lives. Each chapter places parents in the spotlight, inviting educators to hear their voices, consider their perspectives, and recognize the knowledge they possess.

Literacy Practices and Experiences: Many Families, Many Literacies, Many Classrooms

Stuart Greene

One of the key aims of this volume is to connect research focusing on parent involvement in their child(ren)'s education with examinations of family literacy practices, both in and out of the home. In Part II of this book, the authors elaborate upon a set of themes raised by researchers in Part I:

- the importance of attending to local contexts, including the nexus of power, race, class, and gender;
- the necessity of accessing families' funds of knowledge as a means for developing culturally sensitive approaches to teaching and learning;
- the inestimable value of following parents over time to fully grasp parents' abilities to effect changes that benefit their children's lives in the face of seemingly intractable problems.

In developing these themes, the authors in Part II portray the ways in which race, ethnicity, faith, and families' uses of language and different media challenge dominant narratives pervading education reports about family literacy. The stories parents tell, make visible beliefs about literacy and schooling that they convey to their children. Indeed, Auerbach

67

(2002) observes that parents of color "arrive at schools with complex narratives of purposes, possibilities, and disappointments of schooling" (p. 1369). As she explains, parents view the educational process—and their own agency—through the lens of their own experiences. The way parents construe school "mediates their understandings and actions around schooling" (p. 1369). This is a point that Catherine Compton-Lilly underscores when she describes students' commitments to literacy in the first chapter of Part II: What parents value influences what their children believe is important. Despite the public's belief that low-income minority parents are not invested in their children's education, parents want a voice in how their children are educated. However, as Compton-Lilly suggests, the trajectory of student learning is never quite linear, and family literacy, alone, is simply one factor among many that influences children's commitments to school.

A number of researchers have pointed to an apparent disconnect between home and school, and how an increased emphasis on testing and standardization has contributed to this gap. The authors in this part argue that this emphasis limits what educators recognize, value, and foster in terms of literacy. In the pages that follow, researchers complicate our understanding of the relationship between home and school by suggesting that we shift our attention from schools to families. Our understandings of families have been conceptualized narrowly in terms of what constitutes a family, the roles played by various family members, and how changing families will solve educational challenges that children encounter. This tendency is grounded in conventional notions of what counts as "normal" in families.

Caitlin Ryan, among others in Part II, challenges these normalizing tendencies, making the argument that educators must shift their emphasis away from "family literacy" to "literacy of families." Indeed, like the researchers in Part I, the authors in this part challenge a dominant discourse of parent involvement that is universal and that treats difference from the norm as deficit. As they point out, a sociocultural view of family literacy encourages us to consider the historically and culturally situated nature of family structures and the principles that define what it means to be involved. What works for one family at one point in time within a given context will not necessarily work with other families in other contexts, especially when all families do not have access to the same economic and educational resources. For that matter, the notion of family is a highly contested term that Ryan confronts as she discusses the literacy and schooling experiences of children growing up in lesbian, gay, bisexual, and/or transgender (LGBT) families.

The authors in this section also challenge commonsense views of what it means to be literate. Based on observation and interviews, Catherine Compton-Lilly brings into focus the ways in which time affects the meanings that families attach to literacy and how these meanings both evolve and change. Tisha Lewis reveals the moment-to-moment interactions between a mother and child who use multiple literacies—gesture, gaze, *and* text—to construct meaning. As Nadjwa Norton argues, without having the benefit of fine-grained analyses of family literacies, it would be quite easy to ignore the ways children and their families use faith and song to develop a sense of strength needed to transform seemingly painful situations into opportunities for spiritual growth. Similarly, we easily might ignore the rich oral traditions enacted through stories and song that Rosario Ordoñez-Jasis and Susana Y. Flores identified in their work with Mexican American children and families.

The irony of limiting our notions about literacy is that the culturally relevant experiences at home are often more enriching than the skills-based approaches that teachers implement with nonnative speakers of English. Students need to recognize their experiences in the instructional materials teachers use; from a Freirean (1970) perspective, families and teachers need to work collaboratively to define relevant problems and texts that are worth exploring and reading.

The authors in this part also help readers understand how parents and their children move in and out of multiple spaces. For example, participating in events at church, as Nadjwa Norton explains, sheds light on the ways children try to develop a sense of place and identity. Grasping the ways in which low-income underrepresented parents and their children navigate multiple spaces is especially important because their lives are often unstable due to a lack of economic resources. A downturn in the economy and other life choices create conditions of instability and vulnerability. This is especially true of families that encounter unfamiliar sets of beliefs and values in schools that they must navigate without a guidebook.

Not surprisingly, children of immigrant or LGBT families may very well feel out of place, as do children whose families are homeless. Tuan's (1977) distinction between space and place is useful; he explains the threat of unfamiliar spaces and the meaning-making activities that are required to create a sense of place.

> What begins as undifferentiated space becomes place when we get to know it better and endow it with value. . . . The ideas "space" and "place" require each other for definition. From the security and stability of place we are aware of the openness, freedom, and threat of space, and vice

versa. Furthermore, if we think of space as that which allows movement, then place is a pause; each pause in movement makes it possible for location to be transformed into place. (p. 6; quoted in Cresswell, 2004, p. 8)

Families struggle with dislocation, whether it is cultural, psychological, or geographical, and it is a question of how educators help children find places in schools—to develop attachments derived from emotions, history, and memory.

In the end, the authors in Part II raise additional questions that complicate our understanding of the place we call school: What kinds of meanings do families attach to school and to the multiple literacies that surround their lives in and out of school? To what extent do educators provide spaces where children have opportunities to connect the culturally relevant literacies they are immersed in at home with the literate practices privileged in school? To what extent do classroom conversations silence students who may be viewed as different due to gender, class, ethnicity, or race? And what is the psychological effect on children and families when they feel out of place?

These are valuable questions for which there are no clear-cut answers. Still, the implications seem clear: The authors encourage us to revisit commonsense views of family, of literacy, and of how we educate the next generation of teachers.

REFERENCES

Auerbach, S. (2002). "Why do they give the good classes to some and not to others?" Latino parent narratives of struggle in a college access program. *Teachers College Record, 104*(7), 1369–1392.

Cresswell, T. (2004). *Place: A short introduction*. London: Blackwell.

Freire, P. (1970). *Peadgogy of the oppressed*. New York: Continuum.

Tuan, Y. (1977). *Space and place: The perspective of experience*. Minneapolis, MN: University of Minnesota Press.

CHAPTER 5

READING ATTAINMENT OVER TIME

Following Urban Families

Catherine Compton-Lilly

Alicia is in grade 8. Her mother, Ms. Rodriguez, tells me, "Alicia can read her little tail off." She sends Alicia to her room to get the book that she currently is reading. Alicia returns with the book Ruby *(Guy, 2005). It has an African American teenager on the cover. She explains, "I stole it from my brother."*

Peter is also in eighth grade. He identifies J. R. R. Tolkien as his favorite author. He has read all of the books in The Lord of the Rings *series (1954–1955)—some of them more than once. He also continues to read the* Goosebumps *books (1992–1997) that he loved when he was in fifth grade, but still has not read them all. Peter explains, "He [R. L. Stine] wrote just so many."*

Both Alicia and Peter enjoy reading, have found books that resonate with their interests and identities, and identify themselves as avid readers. Both Peter and Alicia are African American and live in the same low-income community. They live with their mothers, neither of whom graduated from high school; both mothers earned a GED. Both students were once members of my first-grade class.

Now in middle school, Peter is doing well, reading above grade level and enthusiastic about school learning. Alicia has tested a year below grade level in reading and finds school-assigned books "boring" and her teachers uncaring. In this chapter, I argue that *both* children are accomplished readers. However, because they are not both meeting school definitions of success, I use the term *literacy attainment* rather than literacy success. Literacy attainment, as I define it here, is the ability to facilely and efficiently use literacy abilities to enact personally relevant and socially shared literacy practices.

COMPLICATING COMMONSENSE VIEWS OF
FAMILIES AND LITERACY

In my research, I have followed Alicia and Peter from my first-grade class-room through middle school. I document not only literacy events in their lives but also the ways in which they have drawn upon the experiences of family members. I examine the role time has played in the construction of literacy practices and introduce the theoretical construct of timescales. After describing Alicia and Peter as readers in middle school, I look back across time to consider the events and contexts that have contributed to their literacy attainment. I focus on ongoing events as well as the meanings that family members bring to their experiences. Finally, I draw conclusions about how literacy success evolves over long periods of time and how longitudinal research can contribute to our understandings of literacy learning in homes and schools.

A NOTE ON METHODS

The cases reported in this chapter were part of an 10-year longitudinal study of eight urban families. At its inception, this 10-year longitudinal study focused on 10 students and their parents. While the original study focused on reading practices, over time it has grown to address a range of issues, including reading identity, official definitions of reading success, and assumptions made about urban families. During the initial phase of the project, the students attended a large urban school that served children from the lowest socioeconomic neighborhood of a mid-sized northeastern city (pseudonym: Cityville); 97% of its students qualified for free or reduced lunch. The participants are African American and Puerto Rican; pseudonyms are used for all participants.

The qualitative longitudinal study described in this chapter incorporates three phases of research, each occurring 3 or 4 years apart. While the initial study involved a rich range of data sources, including interviews, classroom observations, audiotaped class discussions, and student portfolios, the next two phases of the research involved only interviews, writing samples, and reading assessments. During the first and third phases of the project, a cross-case analysis was completed. In the second phase, each family was treated as a separate case. I currently am analyzing phase 4 of the study, data collected with seven of the families when the children were in grades 10 and 11, which I refer to briefly in this chapter's conclusion. For a complete discussion of the methodologies used in this study, I refer the reader to other publications (Compton-Lilly, 2003, 2007, in press).

LITERACY PRACTICES, TIME, AND TIMESCALES

Sociocultural theorists (Gee, 1999; Street, 2005) argue that literacy practices involve sedimented features that accumulate over time. Thus, to understand literacy practices, it is essential to consider the ways in which children operate within time as they learn to read and define themselves as readers and writers. The construct of timescales (Lemke, 2000, 2001, 2007) reveals the multiple temporal worlds people inhabit as well as the connections they make across these temporal worlds. Timescales involve everything from the quick and microscopic changes constantly occurring within the human body, to the days and hours of people's lives, to the slowly evolving geological changes within the universe. The timescale model recognizes the interrelatedness of multiple dimensions of time in people's lives, understandings, and experiences.

Wortham (2006) explores the possibility of using "cross-timescale relations" to understand long-term processes; he describes sets of "linked processes across several timescales" (p. 9) that collectively explain how phenomena occur. Wortham explains that people's identities "thicken" over time, becoming more consistent and established; he argues that academic learning, including literacy development, is related to identity and involves students accessing resources from across various timescales.

In this chapter, I reference literacy practices at three timescales.

Ongoing Timescales. Ongoing timescales reference activities that occurred during the interviews, as well as events that occurred during recent weeks and months in a loosely defined present (e.g., reading particular books, a writing assignment, interactions related to literacy at home or school).

Familial Timescales. Familial timescales reference experiences within families that include the past, present, and future of family members and their personal histories with race, schooling, and literacy. Stories of parents, grandparents, and siblings, along with the children's past experiences, are relevant to the ways the children in this study made sense of literacy and schooling.

Ongoing and familial timescales are contextualized within *historical timescales.* Historical timescales reference larger social and educational histories. At the close of this chapter, I examine how the ongoing and familial accounts documented in this chapter are contextualized within larger historical accounts of people and events.

CAPTURING A MOMENT IN TIME: ALICIA AND PETER AS MIDDLE SCHOOL READERS AND STUDENTS

In this section, I describe Alicia and Peter as literacy learners in middle school. I then consider events and situations that contributed to their literacy attainment and achievement, including their literacy practices across time and the social relationships that surrounded their literacy practices.

Alicia in Eighth Grade

Alicia was simultaneously enjoying books from the *Babysitter Club* series and books she referred to as "love novels." She explained that the latter were "mostly about like sex." She showed me a book called *Ruby*, written by Rosa Guy (2005); its cover featured an African American girl. Alicia explained that she had gotten the book from her brother. She showed me several of her poems and proudly read some of them into my tape recorder.

Ms. Rodriguez reported that Alicia never brought books home from school and never visited the local library. "Alicia's more interested in how she looks now." At the time of the interview, Alicia was reading *The Tell-Tale Heart* (Poe, 1983) in English class. She complained that "it's kinda boring" and "it ain't scary." When I asked her why she thought it was boring, Alicia clarified her response, "I think the story ain't boring, I just think the way my teacher reads it [is boring]." I asked whether they were doing any other reading in school, and Alicia answered, "We ain't doing nothing." By eighth grade, Alicia's friends read only magazines; they didn't read books. She explained that her friends were "just not into it" and that they would rather just "goof around." When asked if reading was fun, Alicia said "no" and claimed that she read only when she was "bored." Alicia tested a year behind in reading.

Peter in Eighth Grade

When Peter was in eighth grade, Ms. Horner, his mother, moved her family to New York City to join her new husband. Peter hated New York and admitted, "When I was down in [New York] I wasn't doing too good [in school]." Peter explained:

I stayed home from school and things 'cause it was like a little
bit too dangerous out there for me. I got into a lot of fights down
there. . . . Like, they would just come across the street and just
start with you. At [Cityville], I never fought.

In New York, Peter attended a magnet school specializing in math, science, and the performing arts; however, it was located in a rough neighborhood. Peter stopped attending school rather than walking to school each morning. However, when Peter returned to his old school in Cityville, he was in danger of being retained in eighth grade based on his low grades. His mother was relieved that he was again attending school regularly and struggled to make sense of the changes that had occurred: "Here he was always doing wonderfully in school. You know, As and Bs. Occasionally he received a C. But just always on the honor roll." She commented that over the years Peter's teachers consistently had been pleased. "Then he comes to New York and unfortunately everything went just downhill." When Peter returned to Cityville, he lived with his father and eventually moved in with his grandmother.

Despite the academic setbacks, Peter continued to be an avid reader. In eighth grade he was "really into" *The Lord of the Rings* books (Tolkien, 1954–1955). He described playing both *Lord of the Rings* board games and video games with his friends. Peter enjoyed most of the books he read at school. His favorite was *Scorpions* (Myers, 1988), a book about two African American brothers.

He explained that his male friends preferred books about sports, while the girls enjoyed fictional stories that dealt with "feelings" and "relationships." He said they got their books from the school library. Although Peter's close friends were readers, he reported that only a few of the students at his school read. Like Alicia, he noted that his peers sometimes gathered to read magazines, and mentioned *Jet* and *Ebony*. He suspected that reading about African American characters was important to kids at his school but he said that he was is not sure why. "They just pay attention more to that kind of stuff." Peter read a ninth-grade text with good comprehension.

DEVELOPING LITERACY PRACTICES ACROSS TIMESCALES

Brief scenes of Alicia and Peter as readers in grade 8 are incomplete and potentially reductive. Taking a longitudinal research approach, and considering timescales, allows us to contextualize how they've developed in their identities as students and readers over time. The following flashbacks into Alicia's and Peter's literacy pasts provide clues about the readers they have become in middle school.

Alicia's Literacy Practices over Time

When Alicia was in first grade, she was an enthusiastic 6-year-old. I remember her being constantly surrounded by friends. In my fieldnotes, I described Alicia and her friends gathering in the book corner each morning to select books to read chorally. When they finished reading one book, they returned to the book corner for another. This continued until the morning bell rang and they gathered around the easel for a story.

When I arrived for the initial interview, Ms. Rodriguez welcomed me to her home. I recorded the following description in my fieldnotes:

> As soon as I mentioned that I was interested in reading, Ms.
> Rodriguez had Alicia's brothers bring out a box of books. The
> box measured about 2 feet by 2 feet and was filled with all sorts
> of children's books that ranged from Dr. Seuss to Little Golden
> Books, board books, and children's novels. Tyreek brought about
> 20 books from his room and, at his mother's request, exchanged
> them for new books from the box. As Tyreek did this, his brothers
> and little sister all gathered around the box to look at the books.
> An older brother, who was about 13 years old, asked for all of the
> Dr. Seuss books. Ms. Rodriguez denied his request, saying he was
> too old for them. Although he argued that he still liked the books,
> Ms. Rodriguez denied his request. Another brother brought out
> his social studies textbook and offered it to Tyreek to read. Tyreek
> took the book readily. As we turned our attention to the inter-
> view questions, Ms. Rodriguez noted that she had another box
> like this in the back.

When I asked Alicia about her favorite books, she identified schoolbooks, *The Itsy Bitsy Spider* (Trapani, 1993) and *One Gorilla* (Morozumi, 1990). Both books were part of our required literature-based basal reading program.

By fifth grade, Alicia was a fan of the *Babysitter's Club* series (Martin & Lerangris, 1986–2000) and had read eight books from the series. I asked Alicia whether there were any Black characters in the *Babysitters* books. She told me that there were but she could not remember their names. When asked if it was important that books have Black characters, Alicia shook her head "no." In addition to the *Babysitters* books, Alicia read books by Judy Blume and still enjoyed her childhood *Winnie-the-Pooh* books. At the time of the interview, she was reading a biography of David Robinson, an African American basketball player. It was around this time that Tyreek brought a biography of Dr. Martin Luther King home from school and Ms. Rodriguez read it aloud to Alicia and her little sister.

However, when I asked Alicia about her favorite books at school, she answered, "None." She reported reading *There's an Owl in the Shower* (George, 1997) and *The Cry of the Crow* (George, 1988). She liked the book *Two Under Par* (Henke, 2005) but responded with "I don't know" when asked about the story. Alicia enjoyed when the writing teacher came to her class; she explained that she and her classmates were collaborating to write scenes for a play.

Alicia's story over time reveals that her relationship to school reading has changed. While in first grade, schoolbooks were her favorites; by fifth grade she did not have favorite schoolbooks and could not remember the plots of the books she read at school. In eighth grade she described her English teacher as "boring." In addition, race became increasingly salient. Although in fifth grade she denied the salience of race, she mentioned texts about African American athletes and Martin Luther King. By eighth grade, Alicia was enjoying primarily love stories about African American teenagers.

While on the surface, Alicia's ongoing experiences resemble a simple chain of events that gradually moves from school storybooks, to series books, to young adult novels, the past operated in complex ways extending beyond a simple accumulation of experiences. The box of books that Alicia's mother collected extended back at least a decade before Alicia was born—when her oldest brother was little. In addition, Alicia's literacy experiences were greatly affected by the extensive literacy practices of her brothers. In her own history, her continued preference for *Winnie-the-Pooh* in fifth grade and the *Babysitters* books in eighth grade marked nostalgia. In addition, there were breaks in established ways of being over time. While her excitement for collaborative reading and writing activities in school faded, her attention to race increased. The development of reading and schooling practices across time were not simple accumulations of experiences. Alicia's current reading practices involved literacy practices that predated her life, selective drawing on her past, and disruptions of previous ways of being a reader and a student.

Peter's Literacy Practices over Time

Peter was a polite, thoughtful young man who actively participated in all first-grade activities. As his mother explained, he was always a "model student." In first grade, Peter owned over 100 books. In eighth grade, he added to his book collection by purchasing books at his school's book fair.

When asked in first grade about reading, Peter reported reading books and the words on the boxes of his video games. By fifth grade, Ms. Horner reported that both her boys went "Pokemon crazy," reading the magazines and cards that accompanied the games. Peter reported that he liked to read horror and mystery books and named R. L. Stine as his favorite author. He had read four *Goosebumps* books (Stine, 1992–1997) and traded these books with his friends. He excitedly described the plot of the book he had just finished. As I got up to leave after our final fifth-grade interview, Peter ran upstairs and returned with the *Goosebumps* book he had just finished and offered it to me recommending that I read it. Exchanging books with friends and passing them on to others was an established social practice for Peter. He also enjoyed reading the *Encyclopedia Brown* books (Sobol, 1963–2007) and explained, "I like the parts when you have to find out stuff." He identified himself as a good reader.

In school, they were reading *James and Giant Peach* (Dahl, 2000) and *The Hundred Penny Box* (Mathis, 1975). Peter noted that he enjoyed the books he read in school and had earned a "B+ or higher." His teacher had the children take turns reading aloud in reading group and then briefly discuss the book. Peter explained, "Sometimes they just ask us, 'How was the book?' 'Do you guys like the book?' She wants to know if it is too hard. That kind of thing." Peter and his classmates regularly completed workbook pages that accompanied the books. "When it is time to do our workbook pages, sometimes she lets us take it home for homework and do them and sometimes we do it together." Peter remained enthusiastic about reading at school and particularly enjoyed projects with his friends. "Well sometimes we have to do like a book report or something, gather up together and we do a report on a book that we all agree on."

By documenting Peter's literacy practices over time, we observe how Peter's early interest in video games and juvenile horror stories evolved into a fascination with *The Lord of the Rings* (Tolkien, 1954–1955). Race did not seem to affect Peter's book choices.

While Alicia experienced a widening rift between her home literacy practices and the literacy practices espoused by the school, Peter continued to value school literacy activities and enjoyed the books assigned by his teachers. Yet, like Alicia, Peter also experienced disjunctures. In particular, his relocation to New York City disrupted his educational record of high grades and almost resulted in his repeating eighth grade. Although he was promoted to grade 9, Peter never regained the A and B averages that he had prior to moving to New York. Over time, we witness this rupture in his educational trajectory alongside the continuity of his interests in Pokemon cards, games, and stories; into series books (e.g., *Goosebumps*, *Encyclopedia Brown*); and eventually into the complex narratives presented in *The Lord of the Rings* series.

FAMILY TIMESCALES: RELATIONSHIPS THAT SURROUND STUDENTS' LITERACY PRACTICES

Familial timescales help us recognize the ways in which people's literacy practices relate to those of their family members. Peter and Alicia draw not only on their ongoing literacy experiences but also on literacy experiences in their families over time. While some of these literacy experiences occurred during their lifetimes, others occurred before they were born and continue to circulate and impact the experiences of family members in the form of stories and memories.

Ms. Rodriguez as a Reader

Alicia's mother was an avid reader. She described reading a range of books connected to her personal and professional life. On a daily basis, she read children's books at the day-care center where she worked and recently used a GED preparation guide to prepare for the GED test. After obtaining her GED, she prepared for her child development associate (CDA) credential and explained that she had been reading books on child development that had not been assigned by her teachers because she wanted to be "above the class." Ms. Rodriguez reported that if she was not asleep by the time she finished her CDA reading, she read a "novel, like a love story or a mystery." In addition, she reported exchanging books with her friends and laughed as she recreated an animated conversation.

"Got a good novel?" "Ahhhhh, did you read so and so, so and so." "No, you got it?" "Yeah. You should check it out." "Send it by so and so or, I come and get it." You know stuff like that.

Ms. Rodriguez's favorite author was Donald Goins, an African American author who wrote about African American characters in urban contexts. She also enjoyed books by Terry McMillan and explained that the protagonist in the book *Mama* (1987) reminded her of herself.

When I read it I was like, this reminds me of me. And he [her high school-aged son] was like, "What do you mean?" I said, "This woman got five kids and struggling and she's all on her own." I said, "I got six. I got more than she do!"

Ms. Horner as a Reader

Peter's mother also identified herself as a reader. When Peter was in first grade, Ms. Horner reported that she loved to read, "because I'm a dreamer and I like to let my mind imagine, just takes me places I wish I could be." Despite the serene image invoked by her description of reading, Ms. Horner enjoyed horror books and mysteries. Ms. Horner was interested in accumulating her "own little library of books"; however, 3 years later, Ms. Horner reported that she was no longer reading novels.

With a new baby, she did not have much time to read but she still enjoyed African American magazines—*Jet*, *Ebony*, and *Essence*.

Ms. Rodriguez's and Ms. Horner's reading practices were established over long periods of time. Notably, it appears that both Alicia's and Peter's reading practices and preferences reflect to varying degrees those of their mothers. Both children read novels for enjoyment and preferred to read books that were similar to those read by their mothers. Like her mother, Alicia enjoyed love novels featuring African American characters. Peter enjoyed mysteries and science fiction, echoing his mother's interests in horror and mystery. However, children do not simply adopt the reading preference practices of parents. Both children adapted their mother's practices in unique ways. While Alicia sometimes borrowed books from her mother, Ms. Rodriguez dismissed Alicia's favorite books as "those novel things." Peter shared his mother's interest in mystery, but also developed a related interest in science fiction. Over time, both children's reading practices and preferences were informed but not restricted by their mother's reading practices.

A GLIMPSE INTO THE FUTURE: PREVIEWS OF SECONDARY SCHOOL CHALLENGES AND GROWTH

Alicia's distancing of herself from school and school literacy activities was apparent in the final phase of this research project. When Alicia was in grade 11, she was reading at the ninth-grade level. School officials believed that Alicia had become a member of a local gang, and following a fight at school she was placed in an alternative program with a modified schedule from December through June of her junior year. Thus, she was not placed in grade 12 when school started in the fall pending the completion of classes that were not available in her modified schedule.

Peter spent his eleventh-grade year in the honors English class where he was enthusiastic about the books he was reading despite his teacher's complaints that he was not working up to his potential. He was earning Bs and Cs in his classes and read successfully at the high school level. However, official notions of school success failed to acknowledge the rich literacy practices of Alicia and Peter as they became competent readers, found books they loved, and assumed identities as readers.

TIME AND SCHOOLING

I argue that both students have achieved a high degree of literacy attainment that has been nurtured within supportive families over long periods of time. However, only Peter was recognized in school as a successful reader. While literacy attainment is marked by using literacy for personal purposes, including entertainment and affiliation with others, school literacy achievement involves official markers of school success, including passing tests, meeting school benchmarks and standards, and fulfilling school criteria for success.

By documenting events at multiple timescales, we begin to recognize the complexities that accompany the ways in which Alicia and Peter constructed themselves as readers over long periods of time. Both Alicia and Peter selectively drew on the stories of family members and their own experiences, while experiencing disjunctures between the past and the present. In addition, they participated in activities and events, and interacted with people and artifacts that brought their own histories of meanings and practices. Time was a critical contextual factor in the ways in which Alicia and Peter made sense of literacy and schooling.

Alicia and Peter also operated within larger historical timescales that referenced historical events known to participants with various degrees of specificity. While participants may not have been able to recount textbook-style details of these social histories, they brought general understandings that were conveyed through the media, school experiences, family stories, and shared cultural knowledge. For African American families living in a low-income urban community, relevant historical timescales included the history of African American people in the United States, histories of urban schooling, historical school literacy practices, and the history of literacy in African American communities.

One of the historical timescales that African American people draw upon is literacy narratives of African American people—the Freedom Schools, biographies of Frederick Douglass, slave narratives, the histories of Black colleges, and the writings of Marcus Garvey, W.E.B. Du Bois, Langston Hughes, and Zora Neale Hurston. In the words and reading practices of Ms. Rodriguez and Ms. Horner, we witness echoes of these accounts. Not only are Alicia, Peter, and their family members recipients of these histories; they are also actors within evolving literacy contexts. However, the ways in which Alicia and Peter draw upon these historical timescales, as well as ongoing and familial timescales, are unique and tied to their individual experiences.

The larger histories of schooling are also relevant. Schools historically have identified texts that count as evidence of literacy success. Traditionally, science fiction and love novels have not been valued in school. While Peter's reading of *The Lord of the Rings* series might be better accepted than Alicia's reading of urban love novels, their readings of these texts are enactments that attest to their literacy abilities and the ways they position themselves relative to schooling.

POSSIBILITIES FOR YOUR CLASSROOM, SCHOOL, AND COMMUNITY

The lessons learned from this study are not simply about the books Alicia read or how Peter's reading practices related to his mother's. The lessons learned are about students' reading practices that go unrecognized and the way children's literacy practices develop over time, and there are steps that educators can take that can make a difference.

- Invite students to talk about their out-of-school literacies and their literate pasts. Talk about books that are important to them and when they found school literacy to be interesting and engaging.
- Stock classrooms and school libraries with books that reflect the experiences and interests of students, even when these texts might not align with traditional school curriculum.
- Have students act as researchers, documenting the various literacy practices in their families. These literacies would include various types of texts (e.g., newspapers, magazines, cookbooks, online texts).
- Have students research the past literacy experiences of family members, documenting the literacy stories of parents, grandparents, and siblings.

These possibilities provide opportunities for students to situate literacy within time and recognize the ways their own literacy practices have developed and changed. In addition, they help teachers to recognize students' and families' literacy practices that otherwise might not have been apparent.

REFERENCES

Compton-Lilly, C. (2003). *Reading families: The literate lives of urban children*. New York: Teachers Collage Press.

Compton-Lilly, C. (2007). *Rereading families: The literate lives of urban children, four years later*. New York: Teachers College Press.

Compton-Lilly, C. (in press). *Time and reading: Negotiations and affiliations of a reader, grades one through eight*. Research in the Teaching of English.

Gee, J. P. (1999). *An introduction to discourse analysis: Theory and method*. New York: Routledge.

Lemke, J. (2000). Across the scales of time: Artifacts, activities, and meanings in ecosocial systems. *Mind, Culture, and Activity, 7*(4), 273–290.

Lemke, J. (2001). The long and short of it: Comments on multiple timescale studies of human activity. *The Journal of the Learning Sciences, 10*(1&2), 17–26.

Lemke, J. (2005). Place, pace and meaning: Multimedia chronotopes. In S. Norris & R. Jones (Eds.), *Discourse in action: Introducing mediated discourse analysis* (pp. 110–122). New York: Routledge.

Street, B. V. (2005). *Literacies across educational contexts: Mediating learning and teaching.* Philadelphia: Caslon.

Wortham, S. (2006). *Learning identity: The joint emergence of social identification and academic learning.* Cambridge: Cambridge University Press.

LITERATURE CITED

Dahl, J. (2000). *James and giant peach.* New York: Puffin Books.

George, J. (1988). *The cry of the crow.* New York: HarperCollins.

George, J. (1997). *There's an owl in the shower.* New York: HarperTrophy.

Guy, R. (2005). *Ruby.* East Orange, NJ: Just Us Books.

Henke, K. (2005) *Two under par.* New York: HarperTrophy.

Martin, A. M., & Lerangris, P. (1986–2000). *The babysitter's club* series. New York: Scholastic Press.

Mathis, S. B. (1975). *The hundred penny box.* New York: Viking Press.

McMillan, T. (1987). *Mama.* Boston: Pocket Books.

Morozumi, A. (1990). *One gorilla.* Hong Kong: Farrar, Straus, & Giroux.

Myers, W. D. (1988). *Scorpions.* New York: HarperCollins.

Poe, E. A. (1983). *The tell-tale heart and other writings.* New York: Bantam Classics.

Sobol, D. (1963–2007). *Encyclopedia Brown* series. New York: Lodestar Books.

Stine, R. L. (1992–1997). *The goosebumps* series. New York: Scholastic Press.

Tolkien, J. R. R. (1954–1955). *The Lord of the Rings* series. Boston: Houghton Mifflin.

Trapani, I. (1993). *The itsy bitsy spider.* Watertown, MA: Charlesbridge.

A RESPONSE TO CHAPTER 5

Stuart Greene

In this chapter, Catherine Compton-Lilly describes an important analytic tool to aid researchers in their efforts to address growth, maturity, change, and even struggle in family literacy practices. The real value of the two cases is the sense that family literacy constitutes just one dimension of Peter's and Alicia's literate lives—a number of factors, including peers and everyday experiences as well as affiliation and dislocation, contribute to children's literate identities. One should not underestimate children's perceptions of place, and particularly Alicia's sense of being out of place in school. In Alicia's case, she resists the kinds of literacies privileged in school, thus creating a sense of struggle, even underachievement, at least in the eyes of her teachers.

The gap between family literacies and school-based practices is evident, and the challenge for teachers is to understand the lives of children who struggle with literacy and schooling, the choices they make, and the sources of their resistance. It is equally important, as others in this volume argue, that as teachers we meet children where they are and widen the lens through which we define literacy.

In the next chapter, Tisha Lewis focuses on the moment-to-moment interactions between a mother and son. In doing so, Lewis brings into focus the relational nature of learning. In addition, she extends our conception of literacy to the ways people make meaning using new technologies.

CHAPTER 6

INTERGENERATIONAL MEANING-MAKING BETWEEN a MOTHER and SON in DIGITAL SPACES

Tisha Y. Lewis

We are a hands-on family. We have to do the task to really, really know it, and by having to do this, it's causing us to work more and more together, which allows our moods to intertwine, interact, and join one another and become unified as one. (Larnee Ali)

Nine-year-old Gerard Ali and I met at an after-school program in 2006. He was a student in my reading class that met twice a week for 35 minutes. It was there that I became introduced to his digital literacy practices as part of his family's literate life. He and his mother, Larnee Ali, both African American, live in an urban neighborhood with two of his brothers. Gerard, a third grader, loves creating comic strips, both on- and offline, engages in online gaming, and interacts with his mother in various digital literacy practices. In each interaction, he shares complex stories through comic strips to make meaning, using verbal and nonverbal descriptions. Through his use of various modes and interactions with others, Gerard engages in intergenerational meaning making.

When Gerard designed his comic strips, my attention was drawn to how he expressed himself using spatial, modal, and linguistic cues. He pointed to and circled characters in print offline and maneuvered the scroll wheel while constantly switching among various windows online. The more I observed Gerard, the more I recognized the significance that semiotic modes (Kress, Jewitt, Ogborn, & Tsatsarelis, 2001) played not only in his designing but also in his communicating and interacting with Larnee.

COMPLICATING COMMONSENSE VIEWS
OF FAMILIES AND LITERACY

Gerard and his mother's interaction demonstrates evidence of an inter-generational thread of learning and multimodality. A complete description of this study is found in other publications (Lewis, 2009, 2010).

This chapter was designed to explore how semiotics (signs and symbols) are related to how Larnee and Gerard communicated with each other through gestures and interactions beyond language (Jewitt, 2003, 2006). Jewitt, who focused on the use of multimodality to explore how various interactional modalities contribute to learning beyond language, and Kenner, Ruby, Jessel, Gregory, and Arju (2008), who examined the role of computers in an intergenerational learning exchange in Sylheti/Bengali-speaking families, provided relevant frameworks for this analysis.

This chapter considers the notion that various modes carry different kinds of information and meaning making that contribute to how individuals learn (Jewitt, 2003, 2006). Nonverbal gestures in close proximity, gazing at the computer screen, as well as what each individual is doing on the computer, and even touching, might play a significant role in intergenerational learning activities (Kenner et al., 2008). At times, Larnee would lean behind Gerard, holding onto the chair while pointing to the screen; sit across from him; or even bend down to stand by his side to understand his designs. She guided their interactions and encouraged his design choices; sometimes she challenged him in this multimodal space. These examples demonstrate how digital literacy practices, though subtle, reflect interactional modalities that lead to new types of technology-mediated learning within homes.

A NOTE ON METHODS

This chapter emerged from an ethnographic case study conducted on the Ali family. Larnee and Gerard live in an urban gentrified community in a highly populated area in a northeastern city. Specifically geared to focal informants Larnee and Gerard, I examined the ways this mother and son engaged and interacted in digital literacy practices in the home for a year. The focus of this study surfaced from literacy/social practices to include family literacy, digital literacy practices, apprenticeships, meaning making, and identities.

Data collection included interviews, participant observations, collecting documents, a guided digital walk through the home, and digital photos. Data analysis involved a grounded theory analysis of transcripts, color coding, fieldnotes, videotapes, and audiotapes to develop categories, themes, and patterns that reflect the intentions of my research questions (Creswell, 1998; Merriam, 2001; Miles & Huberman, 1994). In collecting and analyzing the data, I moved beyond language, which allowed me to focus on Gerard's nonverbal gestures through observations and conversations with him. This interaction included movement, gaze, gestures on the computer or video game (mouse, keys, screen), and talk.

LARNEE AND GERARD'S LITERACY HISTORIES

Larnee does not have her high school diploma, but she did attend school until ninth grade. She entered school at age 12 after her mother was reported to the authorities for child neglect for not enrolling her in school. She remembers teachers telling her that she was the smartest in the class—making As and Bs. Her peers would befriend her to help them cheat. She would never comply and enjoyed learning. While her school life brought joy, her home life was the opposite. Larnee was subjected to horrific acts of verbal, physical, and sexual abuse, and often was confined to her room where she was introduced to technology via television, telephones, and pagers. As an adult, she used new and innovative technological tools (e.g., building a computer, gaming, instant messaging, texting, and talking on her cell phone) and practices that guided and informed her decisions on a daily basis. She enrolled in a computer class; the computer lab became an oasis for learning what made the "computer tick" and to see "how each [piece of] equipment has a role," as well as engaging with her peers in a common practice where she received a great deal of joy and sense of accomplishment. She reflected, "I actually built my own computer from scratch" (Lewis, 2009, p. 69).

Over time, Larnee's management of her family's physical and digital spaces is evidenced by her having a computer in her bedroom to supervise her sons' time on the computer. Here is where homework activities, playtime, lively discussions, and creativity were enacted, and where meaning making was introduced and intensified.

Gerard was born into a two-parent household. He is the middle child of three brothers. Gerard has made As and Bs since he began school but has had difficulties with math fractions. He enjoys reading and asking thought-provoking questions to get to the main idea of a story. In a classroom setting, he might be overlooked because of his quiet and calm demeanor, but as a student in my reading class at the after-school program,

Gerard participated regularly, sharing his thoughts or views on the readings. Gerard enjoyed reading and other literacy practices that highlighted his creativity and ability with digital literacies.

During Spring 2007, while most of the children at the after-school program were outside running around, laughing, and engaging in multiple activities, I observed Gerard involved in discussions about a comic strip that he and his friend Charlie were illustrating. I watched in amazement how this activity superseded all of the other outside practices. I was intrigued by how they spoke about their comics in a cooperative manner. I witnessed how their interactions involved not only language but various forms of actions to communicate information about their comic strip. The boys commented about the sketches, their laughter related to characters, the heavy marks and erasing on the tablet, or their back-and-forth conversations, as they agreed and disagreed about comic strip layouts. When I spoke to Larnee, she explained that for months Gerard had been developing two sets of comic strips on- and offline (computer, hand-drawn) in his black-and-white composition notebook.

Because Gerard was such an avid user of digital literacies, I wondered whether digital literacies were encouraged within the context of his family and whether they were a part of his family's literate life.

CREATING MEANING IN A FAMILY'S DIGITAL SPACE

Meaning making may be interpreted as the relationship between the reader and the text. This meaning depends on what the individual brings to the text, what readers take from texts, and how they make sense of texts (Anstey & Bull, 2006). However, meaning making tends to be less visible in the home. Most families communicate using face-to-face communications and engage in traditional practices in which family members converse with one another (e.g., eating dinner together); however, variations across different kinds of home contexts have not been addressed. Larnee is not yielding these traditional literacy practices in the home, but is concerned about introducing new literacy practices through which the family can communicate better. Family members embrace these modalities as integral parts of their daily lives. Larnee and Gerard found creative ways to communicate face-to-face and beyond face-to-face, through digital tools and texts. They constructed and conveyed personal meaning in how they communicated, which made this practice inaccessible to other families. Larnee and Gerard interacted and engaged in digital literacies in multiple ways, and these interactions shaped the close bond they shared.

During one literacy event, I observed how comfortable Gerard was at the computer designing a comic strip online with Larnee nearby. Gerard spent hours at the computer looking up "sprites" (computer graphic image and animation) online, creating backgrounds or making character choices for his comic. At times, Larnee would sit in a chair, turning to Gerard as the expert to explain his designs to her. At other times, she guided him, asking critical questions, or observing his choices. The interactions in this digital environment were modally dense (Norris, 2004) and pointed to the second-by-second unfolding of meanings that were made in digital environments. For instance, Gerard would shift among multiple screens. He was quick at cutting and pasting blocks or parts of the background from various screens into the comic frame. He took his time to decide which background to use and why. Gerard strategically reshaped backgrounds to fit objects perfectly into the frames.

Gerard believed that these practices were unremarkable, but after observing his discourses, gestures, and meanings, I learned about the intricate abilities that made him an avid and capable digital literacy player, learner, and designer. Understanding his literate identities in a digital environment meant understanding not just what he said or drew but how he chained modes together in complex ways. His world involved a layering of stories—told through images and actions as well as through language—that extended dominant social practices in his home and affected who he was and how he was viewed in on- and offline spaces.

Jewitt (2006) argues that when individuals use "multimodal computer applications, they are engaged with a range of resources and they work with all the modes present on the screen and around it not only from written words and speech" (p. 76). Kress (2000) highlights how the use of the body describes much more than just the engagement or interaction with the computer. If we consider engagement enacted by the way Gerard sits in his chair while maneuvering the mouse, or fixates his eyes on the computer screen, or how Larnee stands over him and the close proximity of their engagement, it is evident that there is meaning behind each touch and movement (Kress, 2000).

During one observation, I noted how Gerard was designing his digital comic strip. He had multiple screens open and was moving back and forth to choose sprites and objects for the background, which he cut and pasted into his comic frame. Standing to his right, Larnee reviewed his comic with him, questioning his design choices.

Larnee: [*Points and circles the comic frames while reading*] I see that he (character from the strip) was on MySpace and he got sleepy and went to sleep . . . and I see where it says, "Five minutes

later." But 5 minutes later what?! What happened five
minutes later?

Gerard: [*Skakes his head*] I'm not that good at doing this.

Larnee: [*With balled fists, softly hits the table*] Yes you are! This is
great!

Tisha: So, Gerard, you put different pieces into one of those
blocks?

Gerard: Yes.

Larnee: Like this Pookeyball. He put that there. [*Talking to me*]
These people . . . he actually added them.

Gerard: Yeah. I'll show you how I got it [*Quickly changes the screen*]

Larnee: Okay, but go back.

Tisha: I would love to see you do that.

Larnee recognized Gerard as a knowledgeable participant in this interaction and pointed out actions that she saw (e.g., "I see that he . . . ," "I
see where it says . . . "). Yet with a high-pitched tone and puzzled look on
her face, she questioned Gerard, "But 5 minutes later what?! What happened 5 minutes later?" Gerard appeared unsure; he shook his head and
explained, "I'm not that good at doing this." Larnee reassured him, "Yes
you are! This is great!" as she simultaneously balled her fist and softly hit
the table. Subtle gestures, close proximity, and focused interactions between mother and son allowed them to create a social space that tended
to each other's needs and displayed camaraderie (Kenner et al., 2008).

In another interaction, Gerard was attempting to download a video on
his site, using Easy Edit (a Web site content editor). He became frustrated,
and at his mother's suggestion, they called his 12-year-old brother Romeo
to assist. In this exchange (see Table 6.1), Larnee attempted to assist Gerard in downloading a video clip.

Notice how Gerard does not speak during this portion of the interaction, but, rather, interacts with gestures. Three things are evident: (1)
Larnee uses touch and proximity to interact with Gerard (frame 3); (2)
Gerard and Larnee use a shared gaze toward the screen and similar gestures (frames 2 and 4); (3) Gerard is being apprenticed by Romeo, on the
phone, via Larnee about how to download the video clip.

Family members do not always have to be in the same room or have
face-to-face interaction in order to communicate or guide one another.
While Larnee was on the phone with Romeo, she tapped Gerard's back to
get him to move out of the chair so that they could switch places. Larnee
would stand next to Gerard during their interactions on the computer.
At times, she stood next to him as support, to assist him with a problem,
or through her curiosity to observe his next move. Each gaze was jointly

TABLE 6.1. Gerard and Larnee Seeking Assistance to Download a Video Clip

	Gerard	Larnee	Gaze	Touch/Action
1	NA	(On phone with Romeo) What is it called that you click on?	Gerard/Larnee look at screen. Gerard has right hand on mouse.	Gerard puts left hand under chin, sitting erect in chair. Larnee puts right hand on table while talking to Romeo on the phone.
2	NA	Click on "What's this?"	Gerard/Larnee look at screen.	Larnee points to the screen. Gerard clicks mouse to screen. Larnee reads the screen with left hand on the arm of the chair.
3	NA	Hold on, wait a second, Gerard.	Gerard/Larnee look at screen.	Larnee lightly taps Gerard's back five times; Gerard leaves chair. Larnee holds chair and sits down holding the phone with hand on mouse.
4	NA	(On phone) I'm not understanding what you're saying.	Gerard/Larnee look at screen.	Larnee's left hand is on the mouse. Gerard puts left hand on the chair arm hunching over to the left with right hand on the table.

Note. Adapted from Kenner, Ruby, Jessel, Gregory, & Arju, 2008.

focused on the screen as they verbally interacted with each other. According to Kenner and colleagues (2008), gazing either at each other or toward a computer screen is another form of communication. Nonverbal gestures are part of how family members establish joint attention while collaboratively creating more complex understandings.

I noticed also that Gerard and Larnee used the same gesture of leaning on the arm chair with their left hand to look at the computer. Larnee mentioned in our first interview that Gerard is the only one of her children whom she saw as a replica of herself. I understood she meant not just that they leaned in the same way toward the screen, but that their interest and investment in what Gerard was producing were shared.

Jewitt (2006) reminds us that "learning is about the design of meaning" (p. 30). Gerard and Larnee shared a bond in how they made meaning multimodally. Their case study demonstrates how such shared family learning in the home can be applied usefully in classrooms and schools, where such 21st-century literacy practices have been lacking.

POSSIBILITIES FOR YOUR CLASSROOM, SCHOOL, AND COMMUNITY

How can the technological tools and mediated learning demonstrated in this study be used to facilitate literacy in the 21st century for students, teachers, and families? For this to occur, schools need to accept, acknowledge, and actively incorporate what students bring with them to the learning settings. It would be ideal for students to share their digital literacy histories and practices in classrooms in ways that are meaningful to them as digital literacy learners, distributors, and producers. For example, students can design a blog or Web site, or create a digital storytelling project about the digital literacy practices their families engage in collectively. Also, teachers can work with families and other community members to create multimodal learning practices in and out of school contexts. For instance, similar to "show-and-tell," teachers can invite a parent to share a distinct digital literacy practice with the class. Families can be encouraged by educators to create digital literacy practices (e.g., blogs, digital calendars, digital comic strips, digital storytelling, and podcasts) to enhance learning—building on their own "funds of knowledge"—in homes and classrooms (Moll, Amanti, Neff, & Gonzalez, 1992). As a result, teachers can use digital literacy practices to encourage and foster agency on the part of students and families; and students, peers, parents, and teachers can engage in interchangeable digital apprenticeships with one another. In this way, students' digital literacy histories and practices will be acknowledged and supported in the classroom as they are at home.

REFERENCES

Anstey, M., & Bull, G. (2006). *Teaching and learning multiliteracies: Changing times, changing literacies*. Newark, DE: International Reading Association.

Creswell, J. W. (1998). *Qualitative inquiry and research design: Choosing among five traditions*. Thousand Oaks, CA: Sage.

Jewitt, C. (2003). Computer-mediated learning: The multimodal construction of mathematical entities on screen. In C. Jewitt & G. Kress (Eds.), *Multimodal literacy* (pp. 34–55). New York: Peter Lang.

Jewitt, C. (2006). *Technology, literacy and learning: A multimodal approach*. London: Routledge.

Kenner, C., Ruby, M., Jessel, J., Gregory, E., & Arju, T. (2008). Intergenerational learning events around the computer: A site for linguistic and cultural exchange. *Language and Education, 22*(4), 298–319.

Kress, G. (2000). Multimodality. In B. Cope & M. Kalantzis (Eds.), *Multiliteracies: Literacy learning and the design of social futures* (pp. 182–202). New York: Routledge.

Kress, G., Jewitt, C., Ogborn, J., & Tsatsarelis, C. (2001). *Multimodal teaching and learning: The rhetorics of the science classroom*. London: Continuum.

Lewis, T. Y. (2009). *Family literacy and digital literacies: A redefined approach to examining social practices of an African-American family*. Unpublished doctoral dissertation, State University of New York at Albany.

Lewis, T. Y. (2010). The motherboard stories. In K. Pahl & J. Roswell, *Artifactual literacies: Every object tells a story* (pp. 112–113). New York: Teachers College Press.

Merriam, S. B. (2001). *Qualitative research and case study applications in education: Revised and expanded from case study research in education*. San Francisco: Jossey-Bass.

Miles, M. B., & Huberman, A. M. (1994). *Qualitative data analysis: An expanded sourcebook* (2nd ed.). Thousand Oaks, CA: Sage.

Moll, L. C., Amanti, C., Neff, D., & Gonzalez, N. (1992). Funds of knowledge for teaching: Using a qualitative approach to connect homes and classrooms. *Theory into Practice, 31*(2), 132–141.

Norris, S. (2004). *Analyzing multimodal interaction: A methodological framework*. London: Routledge.

A RESPONSE TO CHAPTER 6

Stuart Greene

Tisha Lewis provides a unique vantage point in describing the relationship between Larnee and her son Gerard. Not only do we witness them interacting within digital environments, but we also observe how they attach meanings to the moment-to-moment decisions each makes and the ways a simple gaze can influence action. This is an intimate scene between mother and child. While they do not need to be in the same room in order to maintain their relationship, we note how Larnee bends over Gerard to watch, to listen, and to teach. It is difficult not to connect these images of family literacy with the apprenticeship model described by Barbara Rogoff (2003).

Rogoff's research focused on the problem-solving strategies that children acquire through collaboration with knowledgeable adults to complete familiar tasks. The acquisition of problem-solving strategies occurs through what some have called instructional scaffolding: The child observes a given cultural activity modeled by an adult; the child participates in the activity with the aid of the adult, and then carries out the activity alone.

What we witness in this chapter is a similar type of learning that has been absent from the research on both parent involvement and family literacy. Lewis demonstrates how apprenticeship in digital environments can be just as formative as familiar face-to-face interactions. This portrait of learning makes visible the types of involvement that foster learning and support the development of a sense of autonomy that has the potential to facilitate and motivate literacy learning (e.g., Pomerantz, Moorman, & Litwack, 2007). Children like Gerard are able to monitor their own learning and identify sources of information that enable them to solve problems.

In the end, the question that Lewis raises is provocative: Can the type of learning illustrated in this chapter inform classroom instruction? An equally important question involves whether the learning that occurs between mother and son represents, or should represent, the type of learning that children experience in school? Will students be using their technological skills in classrooms to design blogs and Web sites, or create digital storytelling projects? Will teachers work to create multimodal learning practices in and out of school? Might parents be invited to share their digital literacy practices in classrooms?

In the chapter that follows, Caitlin Ryan argues that schools need to seek ways to accommodate differences in family structure as well as students' preferred modalities. She examines differences in the ways in which traditional conceptions of family can silence children from diverse backgrounds. Ryan follows families in a number of different environments: at home, in school, and at other events such as church, sports events, county fairs, arts performances, and community potlucks. Perhaps more than other researchers in this volume, she assumed the role of participant-observer in families' lives.

REFERENCES

Pomerantz, E. M., Moorman, E. A., & Litwack, S. D. (2007). The how, whom, and why of parent involvement in children's academic lives: More is not always better. *Review of Educational Research, 77*(3), 373–410.

Rogoff, B. (2003). *The cultural nature of human development.* New York: Oxford University Press.

CHAPTER 7

TALKING, READING, AND WRITING ABOUT LESBIAN AND GAY FAMILIES IN CLASSROOMS

The Consequences of Different Pedagogical Approaches

Caitlin L. Ryan

When I was a child, one of the reasons I looked forward to second grade was getting to be Student of the Week. When my year finally arrived, I would sit in my classroom and stare enviously at the back table full of toys, rocks, family photos, baby teeth, and sports camp award ribbons from the life of the week's featured child. I couldn't wait to bring in my display, be the center of attention, and get the cards everyone would write me on Friday telling me what they thought of me and my collection.

For me, bringing together my home and school worlds felt exciting and extremely validating. It seemed like a way to connect the best of the different parts of my life all at once into a sort of childhood double bonus: being surrounded by the comforting things I loved from home while still getting to be at school with my friends. Nevertheless, deciding what to include in my display was emotionally wrought. I remember debating over whether or not to make particular parts of my home life public to my peers and carefully weighing the consequences of each decision.

One thing I did not worry about as a child was talking about my family members. My teacher and most of my classmates knew them already, and I had clear language to describe their relationships to one another and their relationship to me: mother, father, brother, grandmother. If I ever have children, however, their Student of the Week experiences and all their other discussions of their lives outside of school will include yet another component to consider: Since I am a lesbian, they will have at least one lesbian mom. In addition to the social pressures that all children have to negotiate in this kind of public performance, my future children will have to decide how and whether they want to label and display their family. My children will not fit a normative model and may have a harder time finding language to use that their peers and teachers will understand.

COMPLICATING COMMONSENSE VIEWS OF PARENTS AND COMMUNITIES

The good news is that my future children will hardly be alone in their experiences. Although firm numbers are hard to come by, estimates suggest there are somewhere between 6 and 14 million children in the United States with at least one lesbian, gay, bisexual, and/or transgender (LGBT) parent (Patterson, 1992), with best current estimates around 10 million. While there have always been children with LGBT parents (some believe even the archetypic lesbian poet Sappho had a daughter named Cleis), for many decades most of these children were born in the context of heterosexual marriages before one or both members of the couple came out as lesbian, gay, bisexual, and/or transgendered. Beginning in the early 1990s, however, there was a so-called lesbian baby boom (Patterson, 1992; Patterson & Redding, 1996; Tasker & Golombok, 1997) or "gayby boom" (see Jennings, 2008, and http://www.wordspy.com/words/gayby-boom.asp), with babies born into LGBT-headed families. With increasing rights and visibility for LGBT people, friendly adoption laws in some states, and more reproductive technologies available, gay couples frequently are choosing to have children together. And even though LGBT people historically are undercounted because it is not always safe to be out, research from the 2000 Census shows that gay and lesbian couples live in 99.3% of *all* counties in the United States (Gates & Ost, 2004).

LGBT-headed families are of all races, in all socioeconomic categories; they are single, partnered, married, divorced, or in other types of relationships. They have children through assisted reproduction, surrogacy, straight relationships, foster care, or adoption, either domestic or international. They may be religious or not, monoracial or multiracial, disabled or able bodied, publicly out or not out. They may be custodial parents or noncustodial parents. LGBT families reside in all states and send their children to all types of schools, so to serve the educational needs of all students, all schools have to be prepared to work with LGBT families.

A NOTE ON METHODS

For over a year I have been working with five diverse lesbian-headed families in a midwestern city to document the community and school contexts in which children grow up and to better understand the experiences of these families as they navigate multiple spaces, including their children's schools. My research was a multisite ethnography, which involved prolonged participant-observation, informal interviews with the participants, and the collection of documents and other artifacts. I asked the children of these families to be "teachers" who "helped me with my homework." They loved teasing me that I was still in school just like them (21st grade, according to our calculations!), and they enjoyed teaching me what it was like to be a kid from their perspective.

I spent time with the families, in particular the children, at home, in school, and at other events such as church, sports events, county fairs, arts performances, and community potlucks over the course of 14 months. I gave rides to school and babysat when the moms needed a break. I accompanied each child at school for several days each week over a 3-week period in the spring and then again for a few days in the fall in their new classrooms. Over the summer I gathered most of the children for a book club where they got to know one another and where we read and discussed books that represented diverse families. In total I worked with eight moms, 11 elementary school-aged children, and 15 teachers.

LGBT PARENTS AND THEIR CHILDREN'S SCHOOLS

Like others, these families experienced some tensions and frustrations while navigating their children's schools. In our conversations, they shared stories of tears when a child's friend wasn't allowed to come over, frustration when forms had to be rewritten continually to encompass their family structure, and weariness at having to explain yet again that, yes, you really could have two moms and, no, elementary school wasn't too early to talk about lesbian-headed families. These parents' experiences echo general findings of other studies of LGBT parents in schools (e.g., Bowers, 2008; Casper & Schultz, 1999). As a whole, LGBT parents know that schools could make changes at an institutional level to better welcome their families (Casper & Schultz, 1999; Kissen, 2003; Lamme & Lamme, 2001), just as they could make changes to welcome parents of other marginalized groups, as documented in several chapters of this book.

THE LITERACY OF FAMILIES:
HOW PARENTS ARE PRESENTED IN THE CURRICULUM

A good deal of negotiation around families occurred when parents weren't physically present at schools. To account for all the ways that families are involved with schools, we must think not only about volunteering or participation in parent–teacher conferences, but also about how families are discussed and described in classrooms. This is what I call the "literacy of families"—all the ways that families are read, written, and talked about—in curriculum for young children. For children from LGBT families, the literacy of families means that reading, writing, and speaking involve contested spaces where they continually must negotiate the visibility of their family. It is through the pedagogical approaches of teachers that information about LGBT families becomes visible or hidden within classrooms. This shift in thinking from family literacy to literacy of families is important because it centers the choices of children from LGBT families within the ongoing daily flow of classroom activity rather than via agreements between parents and teachers that might not involve the child(ren). Thus, children of all ages with LGBT parents are most directly responsible for mediating daily negotiations in schools.

I draw on my larger study to illustrate ongoing social negotiations around the literacy of families. Specifically, I detail two dissimilar experiences with classroom pedagogy and curriculum that two little girls with lesbian mothers, Mary and Mallory (all names are pseudonyms), experienced as first graders. First, I provide historical and contemporary context on the state of LGBT families. Then, I discuss the pedagogical approaches of the girls' two teachers and the different kinds of discussions about families that these different approaches permitted. I end the chapter by asking teachers to reflect on the unintended consequences their pedagogies may have for children from diverse families, including children with LGBT parents.

Historical and Current Perspectives on LGBT Families

Reflecting on the daily realities faced by American LGBT families, Casper and Schultz (1999) write, "Our world is enveloped by an atmosphere of discrimination, with its attendant consequences of guilt, fear, and hatred. It shouts at parents and children to keep their lives secret" (p. 16). In spite of recent modest legal and cultural gains, LGBT issues of all types are still highly divisive and hotly contested (e.g., California's Proposition 8, the military's Don't Ask, Don't Tell policy). Because some outside the LGBT community tend to equate being LGBT with sex and sexual acts rather than with relationships, emotions, and interpersonal connections, issues related to raising children become particularly sensitive. And because of the propagation of myths connecting gay men to pedophilia and suggesting that LGBT people keep their community alive by "recruiting" children to be gay, many inherently distrust gay adults who spend time around children, despite how thoroughly disproven these claims may be. LGBT parents and their children begin their journeys as families surrounded by these specters and stereotypes (Garner, 2004). Furthermore, despite contrary evidence, there is deep-seated suspicion that LGBT parents will "make" their children gay. Yet "research has shown that the adjustment, development, and psychological well-being of children is unrelated to parental sexual orientation and that children of lesbian and gay parents are as likely as those of heterosexual parents to flourish" (APA, 2004, quoted in Patterson, 2006, p. 243; also see information disseminated by the American Bar Association, the American Medical Association, the American Academy of Pediatrics, and the American Psychiatric Association).

Nevertheless, discrimination persists. A recent study by GLSEN (Kosciw & Diaz, 2008) confirmed that students with LGBT parent(s) hear negative comments and messages about their families in schools. Specifically, 53% of LGBT parents feel excluded from their child(ren)'s school, 22% of students said that an educator had discouraged them from talking about their family at school, and 36% of students felt that school personnel did not acknowledge their LGBT families. Sexuality remains a hidden type of diversity, especially in elementary schools where children with LGBT parents are left to navigate this silence.

Mary's Experiences at School

"You know what you're going to learn today? That I'm a lot like other kids."
—Mary, first grader with two lesbian mothers

Mary Jensen, a first grader in a large midwestern city, arrives for another morning at her small, private, religiously affiliated school. She puts her coat and backpack in their designated places and smoothes out her school uniform before sitting down at her desk. She carefully arranges her pencils on her desk top before finding a book for silent reading. Mary and I have played together at her house before, where we talked in detail about her life with her sister and her two lesbian moms. Today, my first day visiting her at school, I pull a chair up next to her desk and sit with her, my notepad and pen on my lap. Soon, we will stand with the other students and dutifully recite both the Pledge of Allegiance and the Pledge to the Christian flag, affirming themselves as members of the Kingdom of Christ before beginning the lessons of the day. Now, though, before Mary begins reading, she turns to me and whispers softly, "I'm a lot like other kids."

Mary's School, Teacher, and Classroom. Mary attends a private, suburban, traditional, religiously affiliated elementary school. Her first-grade teacher, Ms. Porter, was in her final year of teaching before retirement. She attended a religiously affiliated college, received her teaching credentials through that religious denomination, and had always taught in religiously affiliated schools. A dedicated teacher, Ms. Porter is deeply invested in the school/church community. For example, she always greets parents by name. Ms. Porter defines her pedagogical methods as "traditional." She told me: "I'm comfortable with what I do. If somebody else doesn't like it, then . . . " Although she believes in traditional teaching, she sometimes uses current education discourse to support her practices. As she told me, "New ideas don't make sense to every person. . . . For example, I call [my approach] reading workshop, but somebody else might look at it and say, 'what?'"

These traditional beliefs and teaching methods led Ms. Porter to create what could be called a teacher-centered pedagogy. In her classroom, students were supposed to learn the information presented by Ms. Porter. They were expected to recall information quickly and precisely within traditional initiation–response–evaluation structures (e.g., Cazden, 2001). In lessons, Ms. Porter would review information repeatedly so students learned the exact words and facts required. As is common in teacher-centered classrooms, the focus was on knowledge, not on process.

With these expectations, there was very little room for student imagination or experimentation. The class writing workshop, for example, consisted of doing things such as underlining the rhyming words in a poem or copying a poem over in the student's best handwriting. Ms. Porter's responses to students highlighted her pedagogical control. Ms. Porter often would not continue class until a student could produce the exact label she had taught previously, even if the concept the child was expressing was similar to the one being sought. One time, when a student asked if he could play his own songs on a musical instrument during music time, she simply responded, "No." Even when doing some work around mental imagery of a poem, Ms. Porter directed, "Imagine . . . riding a tricycle. I'll tell you what to do [i.e., what to imagine]."

Ms. Porter's emphasis on content knowledge actually discouraged the children from making connections to other parts of their lives—like family. The few times when she did allow space for these comments, Ms. Porter often would put a particular limit on the conversation. For example, one time, when several students were raising their hands to talk, she said, "Some of you have comments. . . . I will take three." After each student's contribution to the conversation, Ms. Porter simply responded, "OK," and then called on the next student. Other times, she would tell students to "rest your arms," which meant she wasn't going to take any comments so they should put their arms down. Once, a student began a story, saying, "A funny thing happened when I was a baby . . . " Ms. Porter quickly interrupted and redirected the class back to academic work, saying, "We're not going to talk about that because we're going to stay focused on our sentences." For students who insisted on sharing without Ms. Porter's invitation, there were negative consequences and loss of privileges.

Not everything about students was discouraged, however. Christian stories, themes, and messages formed a dominant discourse in the classroom that Ms. Porter accepted. The class recited the Pledge to the Christian flag every morning, and had daily Bible study (including verses to memorize) and weekly chapel services. Many religious books were available for reading, and children's art projects depicted religious scenes. Since Mary and her family belong to the church with which the school is affiliated, this is a discourse that Mary can and did participate in fully and equally.

What This Means for Mary. Ms. Porter's pedagogical control, silencing of student input, and foregrounding of religious identity means Mary can participate in the social world of the classroom equally even though information about her lesbian-headed family is silenced. In other words, Mary does not talk about her family at school, but neither does anyone else in her class, generally. Ms. Porter's pedagogical approach shuts down the curricular inclusion of families, but, perhaps ironically, this isn't all bad for Mary as a child with lesbian mothers. While I never heard Mary speak about her two moms, or use the terms of address she uses for her moms, while at school, the only information I heard other children mention about their families was whispered between friends or talked about on the playground. For all intents and purposes then, there was no explicit literacy of families in Ms. Porter's classroom. Mary received positive attention when she answered questions about the Bible, kept trying without giving up, and did her work quietly. The result was that Mary participated happily in the shared religious discourse that stressed her commonality with other students.

Mallory's Experiences at School

"Who is that holding you [in that picture]?"
"Huh? That's my other mom."
— Mallory, first grader with lesbian mothers, to a peer

Mallory Winston, another first grader in a very different school environment from Mary, takes her place at the front of the classroom in the
chair usually reserved for her teacher. She adjusts her glasses nervously
as her classmates in this suburban public school gather on the carpet at
her feet. Mallory is holding a large poster dotted with colorful photo-
graphs and words written in her best first-grade handwriting. This is her
VIP week, the time she has been assigned to share her personal story and
family timeline project with her class. The paper contains pictures from
her life, starting with her birth in China, her adoption, and her move to
the States. It also has pictures of her two adoptive extended families, one
White and one ethnically Chinese. She walks the class through many of
these images and has gotten through a number of these details, but has
yet to point out that she was adopted by two women and therefore has
two lesbian moms. As she is talking, a student asks about a picture farther
down the page. Mallory responds, "That's my other mom."

Mallory's School, Teacher, and Classroom. Mallory attends a public elementary school in a wealthy, predominantly White suburb. Her teacher,
Mrs. McConnell, works to establish a caring, respectful learning community. For example, she addresses her students as "friends" and encourages them to do the same. Her students get to choose their own reading
and writing topics, frequently share work with peers, and develop writing
workshop pieces over time and several drafts. Students in Mrs. McConnell's class also are assigned a "VIP week" where they get to share their
personal stories with the class and bring in important items from home
for show-and-tell (much like my own second-grade Student of the Week
experience).

Mrs. McConnell's approach creates what could be called a student-
centered pedagogy. She is committed to fostering students' identities as
learners, referring to her students as "writers" or "readers" or "scientists."
She frequently reminds students that "there are many ways to solve a
problem," and asks, after one student has shared his or her approach,
"Whose brain did it a different way?" This multiplicity is expected, and
the different individual processes students take to get to an answer are
valued. Knowledge often is constructed by drawing on experiences that

students have outside of school, and Mrs. McConnell's responses highlight connections between home and school learning. For example, as part of the morning routines, the students discuss weather patterns and temperatures. Mrs. McConnell asks the students, "What did your bodies feel this morning as you walked to school?" These contributions are important to the learning in the classroom, and she praises students when they share stories related to the topic of study. When such stories are shared in relation to a book the class is reading, Mrs. McConnell even labels these comments "text–self" connections.

Students' identities as current and future learners are a dominant discourse in the classroom. For example, Mrs. McConnell, when modeling good peer-editing support for writers, will say, "As a reader, I'm wondering . . . " She reminds students that "smart kids check their work," and together the class creates a list of 12 characteristics of scientists. As with the discourse of Christian themes and images in Mary's classroom, this discourse of learners' identities is a discourse that Mallory can and does participate in fully and equally. For example, Mallory is called a "scientist" and "Chinese expert" (because of her knowledge of language and culture gained from traveling to China and attending Chinese school) by her teacher and peers.

Other expectations of students, however, cause a bit more difficulty for Mallory. As mentioned, students in Mrs. McConnell's class are expected to share about their lives outside of school as part of their growth as academic learners. As Mrs. McConnell told them, "You are the experts on yourselves." These expectations to talk about family and life outside of school were most obvious in the family project and the turn at being VIP for a week. During Mallory's VIP week, she, as required, shared her personal/family timeline with the class. As she shared, she had to negotiate levels of personal exposure in explaining the different features of her timeline. Although she was clear and matter-of-fact about several parts of her life, including her adoption from China and her multiracial family, she did not actually mention her lesbian moms on her own, until prompted by a peer. Conversation about her moms was made even more difficult because of the pain of her adoptive moms' recent separation. Mallory eventually explained to her class that Chen is her "other mom's last name . . . she got divorced in our family," and Mallory no longer saw her on a regular basis. Mallory's mother's new girlfriend was included with Mallory in a few photos, and Mallory described her as "my friend, Amanda."

Other information proved even harder to negotiate. For example, during question and answer time, a student pointed to a photo of Mallory's extended family and asked her, "Who is your dad? In that picture?" Mallory responded, "I don't have a dad, actually." This same boy immediately asked another question, trying to make sense of this information: "Did he die?" In his experience, not having a dad likely meant having had one and losing him, but in Mallory's family of two moms, there was no such loss. Mallory doesn't have a dad simply because she doesn't; she has lesbian moms. After this boy's question, however, there was only silence; neither Mallory nor Mrs. McConnell said anything, and another student was called on to ask the next question. Therefore, despite Mallory's attempts to publicly account for her family, Mrs. McConnell failed to mediate this conversation for her students. Her uncertainty, however motivated, effectively reinforced silences around lesbian-headed families.

What This Means for Mallory. Again, there's a tension for Mallory, although perhaps slightly less obvious than the one in Mary's classroom. In Mallory's classroom, Mrs. McConnell's pedagogical openness, her invitations for student input, and the foregrounding of personal identity means that Mallory has opportunities to discuss the details of her family structure in the classroom. The facts of her family, including her race, her adoption status, and her moms, are talked about, and therefore validated, within the formal structure of the required curriculum. In many ways, this is great news that works directly against the silencing experienced by so many (Kosciw & Diaz, 2008). There are no doubt many LGBT parents who would be thrilled to be part of an environment as accepting as this classroom, and many children from LGBT-headed families who would feel affirmed and validated by this VIP exercise. However, it seems important to note that participation in this literacy of families event is mediated nearly entirely by Mallory herself, in front of her entire class, and therefore requires significant social risk.

POSSIBILITIES FOR YOUR CLASSROOM, SCHOOL, AND COMMUNITY

I present these two distinct teaching styles knowing that they are, in many ways, polar extremes. I do not want to suggest that one approach is good and one is bad, and that all teachers must start doing some particular thing to be more welcoming to children with LGBT parents. Instead, I hope that sharing the complicated experiences of children from lesbian-headed families within both of these classrooms serves as an acknowledgment of the potentials and limitations of the many various approaches for children with LGBT parents. For many communities, asking children to bring their home and family lives into school may be an important, equitable, empowering process, but for children with LGBT parents, their family lives are what is stigmatized in the first place, so this "solution" becomes more complicated. On the one hand, silences can be stifling, yet they can provide cover from unwanted exposure. Children are sensitive to feeling different, and there are many times when they won't want their parents' (or parent's) sexuality to impinge on and interfere with their own social worlds. On the other hand, opportunities to speak openly and honestly about those one loves can be liberating, yet actually can create an unsafe space by requiring exposure. This is especially difficult when the burden falls solely on the child. As Abigail Garner (2004) reminds us, "To children, careful discretion about their parents is neither about identity nor about politics; it is about acceptance and safety" (p. 121). Absent any planning or mediation between family members, teachers, and students ahead of time, it is children of LGBT parents who are left to navigate this balance of visibility and social risk.

So, what middle ground might be possible to support LGBT families in mediating this balance of openness and safety? First of all, we can recognize and respect children's right to come out about their families to those people at those times that they choose (COLAGE, n.d.; Garner, 2004; Tasker & Golombok, 1997). That means creating an open and supportive environment so children are welcome to share but are never required to share. Such a space would require teachers to become more aware of all the ways that their pedagogical approach allows students' home and family lives to enter into the school day.

Preliminary findings from other data in my study suggest that children with lesbian mothers will tailor their use of labels and pronouns in their writing assignments based on how public they believe their writing will be. Given this finding, teachers could guide students in considering their audience as they work on a particular piece of writing. They also could allow students to choose writing topics, and to write in a private journal or mark a particular piece of writing as private. Journals that circulate between parents at home and the children at school may be private, familiar spaces of writing that might be especially appreciated by LGBT-headed families.

Second, teachers could ensure that their discussions of families focus on a wide range of human experiences, thereby contextualizing discussion of LGBT-headed families in larger discussions of family diversity. This would give children with LGBT parents an opportunity to share about their families, while also giving them the support of standing alongside their peers who also might have "untraditional" family arrangements. Finally, teachers could discuss LGBT people, including LGBT-headed families, even when they do not have a child with same-sex parents in their classroom. Speaking openly and honestly about LGBT issues in developmentally appropriate ways, whether through literature (Albright & Bedford, 2006; Hermann-Wilmarth, 2007; King & Schneider, 1999) or through other curricular connections (Chasnoff et al., 1996), helps all students be prepared to encounter the full diversity of our world.

No matter what specific actions are taken, the experiences of Mary and Mallory demonstrate that the pedagogical approaches of teachers shape information students either can or must bring with them to school to be successful learners in that environment. Family involvement extends far beyond conference days and field trips; it permeates elementary school curricula. If teachers are ready to mediate classroom conversations, respect children's own choices, foster collaboration between teachers and parents, and discuss a wide variety of family types, children with LGBT parents will be able to *both* honestly acknowledge their family members and still feel, as Mary said, "a lot like other kids."

Author's Note: The author thanks the families and teachers who worked with her, as well as Mollie Blackburn and Audra Slocum for their feedback during the development of this chapter.

REFERENCES

Albright, L., & Bedford, A. (2006). From resistance to acceptance—introducing books with gay and lesbian characters. *Journal of Children's Literature, 32*(1), 9–15.

Bowers, L. A. (2008). Standing up for diversity: Lesbian mothers' suggestions for teachers. *Kappa Delta Pi Record, 44*(4), 181–183.

Casper, V., & Schultz, S. (1999). *Gay parents/straight schools: Building communication and trust.* New York: Teachers College Press.

Cazden, C. B. (2001). *Classroom discourse* (2nd ed.). Portsmouth, NH: Heinemann.

Chasnoff, D., Cohen, H. S., Bowman, B., Lyman, K., Coates, K., Yacker, F., et al. (1996). *It's elementary: Talking about gay issues in school.* Harriman, NY: New Day Films.

COLAGE (n.d.) COLAGE: About us. Retrieved November 15, 2009, from www. colage.org/about/

Garner, A. (2004). *Families like mine: Children of gay parents tell it like it is.* New York: HarperCollins.

Gates, G. J., & Ost, J. (2004). *The gay and lesbian atlas.* Washington, DC: Urban Institute Press.

Hermann-Wilmarth, J. (2007). Full inclusion: Understanding the role of gay and lesbian texts and films in teacher education classrooms. *Language Arts, 84*(4), 347–356.

Jennings, K. (2008). Understanding the gayby boom: LGBT parents and independent schools. *Independent School, 68*(1), 91–93.

King, J., & Schneider, J. (1999). Locating a place for gay and lesbian themes in elementary reading, writing, and talking. In W. Letts & J. Sears (Eds.), *Queering elementary education* (pp. 125–136). Lanham, MD: Rowman & Littlefield.

Kissen, R. M. (Ed.). (2003). *Getting ready for Benjamin: Preparing teachers for sexual diversity in the classroom.* New York: Rowman & Littlefield.

Kosciw, J. G., & Diaz, E. M. (2008). *Involved, invisible, ignored: The experiences of lesbian, gay, bisexual and transgender parents and their children in our nation's K–12 schools.* New York: Gay, Lesbian and Straight Education Network.

Lamme, L., & Lamme, L. (2001). Welcoming children from gay families into our schools. *Educational Leadership, 59*(4), 65–69.

Patterson, C. J. (1992). Children of lesbian and gay parents. *Child Development, 63,* 1025–1042.

Patterson, C. J. (2006). Children of lesbian and gay parents. *Current Directions in Psychological Science, 15,* 241–244.

Patterson, C. J., & Redding, R. (1996). Lesbian and gay families with children: Public policy implications of social science research. *Journal of Social Issues, 52,* 29–50.

Tasker, F. L., & Golombok, S. (1997). *Growing up in a lesbian family: Effects on child development.* New York: Guilford Press.

A RESPONSE TO CHAPTER 7

Stuart Greene

Caitlin Ryan's story of Mary and Mallory is a narrative about contested spaces, where children from LGBT families must negotiate differences in their classrooms each day. The threat of difference in schools manifests itself in policies that silence students. While silencing is often most visible in ESL classrooms where students are prevented from speaking their native language, it is also evident in Catherine Compton-Lilly's portrait of Alicia, which demonstrates how differences can marginalize students. For children from LGBT families, silencing can be devastating as students like Mary and Mallory interact with dominant narratives that reify traditional conceptions of family, kinship, social relationships, gender, and sexuality.

Silence can mean many things in classrooms. It can be productive as students resist participating in politically charged conversations that exclude diverse points of view. As Schultz (2009) argues, silence can serve as protection for children like Mary and Mallory. By choosing to be silent, they can reveal what in their home life they want to be public about and "when to shroud those topics in silence, keeping them separate from school" (p. 29). In the end, Schultz explains that silence represents many students' "logical response to complex, politically charged situation[s]" (p. 33).

It may seem logical to provide spaces for children from LGBT families to participate in conversations about their experiences. However, Ryan makes clear that the very nature of these children's experiences is what makes them vulnerable in the first place. Thus the question becomes how teachers can foster discussion about sensitive topics in productive ways—where students not only talk about difference, but enact tolerance for differences in their everyday lives. Ryan challenges teachers to examine the source of children's silence, recognizing that silence can be a productive stance of refusal, resistance, and power.

One key question is, What, as teachers, is our responsibility in allowing some students to speak and allowing others to remain silent? This type of question prompts us to examine more fully the distinction Ryan makes in her story of Mallory and Mary—between family literacy and literacies of families.

She also points out that teachers can use children's questions—however naive or misdirected—as moments for instruction. This is apparent in the case when a child asks Mallory if her father died. Neither Mallory nor the teacher knows how to answer the question. Indeed, the teacher could have explained that family structures vary and that not all children have a father and mother. The alternative explanation is not that the father died, but that Mallory has two moms.

In the next chapter, Nadjwa Norton picks up on the challenges that teachers face, especially in a public school setting. Her focus on faith provides a unique context for understanding the gap between the literacies of home and school and the ways in which teaching can silence students. The children in Norton's study express their faith through song, through prayer, and through the relationships they forge with one another. Their faith enables them to achieve a sense of agency in ways that school-based literacies do not. Like Alicia in Compton-Lilly's chapter and Mary and Mallory in Ryan's chapter, the children in Chapter 8 must navigate multiple spaces and literacies that can be either inclusive or marginalizing.

REFERENCE

Schultz, K. (2009). *Rethinking classroom participation: Listening to silence.* New York: Teachers College Press.

GOD'S PEOPLE ARE STRONG

Children's Spiritual Literacy Practices

Nadjwa E. L. Norton

What a mighty God we serve
Angels bow before him
Heaven and earth adore him
What a mighty God we serve

This verse hails from a well-known gospel song entitled *What a Mighty God We Serve*. As a Black female whose spiritualities are grounded in African American Christianity as well as Islam, and Native American spiritualities, I recall in my childhood how I belted these lyrics out, keeping time with a tambourine, in devotion at Pentecostal churches. More recently, I sang this song as a participant-observer when I visited the churches of two of my research participants, and on one Saturday afternoon at the home of Kevin, 6 years old, and Rhonda, his 4-year-old cousin/sister. Rhonda was biologically Kevin's cousin. However, the family's culture maintained that because both nuclear families lived together in an apartment as a family, they would interchange calling each other sister/brother/cousin.

This song represents a cornerstone tenet of Black spiritualities: that God is mighty, strong, and omnipotent. This tenet has been acknowledged and celebrated in African American culture. Throughout time, these beliefs have been incorporated into music and have spurred Blacks to deeper spirituality, passing along spiritual knowledge across generations and within a larger community, supporting perseverance against obstacles, and inspiring new visions of progress, fortitude, and perseverance (Hull, 2001).

The careful articulation of the tenet, God is mighty, has been explored most expansively in the fields of theology and spiritualities, where many, including Mitchem (2002), contend that attending to spiritualities and

111

spiritual practices must include "how we communicate with God and how we communicate about God" (p. 38). Combining sociocultural perspectives and spirituality connects literacy to minds, spirits, and bodies.

COMPLICATING COMMONSENSE VIEWS OF PARENTS AND COMMUNITIES

This chapter contributes to closing a gap in literacy research by illustrating how children enact spiritual literacy practices by reading and writing texts. In so doing, children name God as an integral member of their family. As they draw on resources in their family to help themselves, they enact diverse spiritual literacy practices on a daily basis, relating to God as both part of the belief system of their family and an actual member of their family.

Commitment to sociocultural understandings of literacy practices entails incorporating the notion that people read, write, listen to, and speak oral, gestural, behavioral, visual, media, body, and print texts (Gallego & Hollingsworth, 2000). This expanded definition of text consists of anything that has meaning, not just print. Furthermore, reading becomes defined as making meaning of text, and writing means bringing text into existence (Freire & Macedo, 1987). Thus, examining people's literacies, including their spiritual literacies, consists of documenting the ways people interact with texts, including people, such as teachers and family members; (un)seen forces, such as God; and classrooms, homes, or churches.

Increasingly, critical sociocultural theorists argue that people must adhere to the ways in which constructs of power limit or provide access to literacies, tools, resources, and identities (Lewis, Enciso, & Moje, 2007). This tenet requires analyzing the macro- and micro-level aspects of power that move across communities and systems.

Such understandings of power bring forth an indispensable tenet of agency. Agency encompasses the ways in which people utilize literacies to rename and remake themselves within embedded relations of power (Lewis et al., 2007). In tracing deeper currents of agency, it becomes important to note that people who enact agency have not accepted their current situations. They have alternative visions, believe in their abilities to shape communities as well as be shaped by them, and understand that power flows in multiple directions (Freire, 1998). Despite this contribution of the tenet of agency, there is still the tendency to place agentic notions in the hands of adults rather than children (Norton, 2005). This focus denies the myriad of ways that children enact literacy practices to negotiate and remake their worlds.

This focus is particularly important in light of the misinformation that teachers have concerning the separation of church and state. Many teachers believe that spiritualities can't be discussed or honored in the classroom. However, legally teachers are able to discuss and honor people's spiritualities. They may not proselytize and convert. Yet, fear of legal ramifications and the taboo nature of spiritualities complicates the situation, leading to circumstances that prevent many teachers from seeing the ways in which schools already validate some spiritualities above others and silence children who may not have spiritual beliefs or who are a part of marginalized or lesser known spiritualities. For example, children who are part of Judeo-Christian religions often have their spiritualities acknowledged and incorporated in schools. Others, whose spiritualities may include Buddhist religions, connections to nature, or acceptance of same-sex family relationships, may be ostracized, ignored, or penalized. In such cases the spiritual identities that are integral to people's literacies are overlooked, misunderstood, and/or constructed in deficit.

A NOTE ON METHODS

This study was designed to focus on literacy practices and spiritual practices of first-grade Black and Latina/o children who attend a New York City public school, and their similar-aged brothers, cousins, and other family members observed in home and church settings (Norton, 2009). The study sought to document how the literacy and spiritual practices led to equities and inequities within the classroom. For example, did children's spiritualities provide them access to more or less resources, better or worse relationships with the teacher, and opportunities to have more or less meaningful connections to classroom content and learning experiences? This narrative inquiry took place outside of school.

This chapter focuses on Gabe, a 6-year-old Black/Puerto Rican boy, Kevin, a 6-year-old Black/Ghanaian American boy, and Joseph, Kevin's 7-year-old Black/Ghanaian American cousin/brother.

The children participated in four semistructured interviews, and as co-researchers in focus groups where they discussed common topics such as family involvement, literacy practices, and spiritual practices. Additionally, they engaged in collaborative conversations, a method where they participated in curricular discussions and planning with the teacher and the researcher. Throughout these experiences, the participants created artifacts that involved taking pictures, gathering collages, drawing, selecting spiritual cards, and making wood sculptures. Finally, I shadowed each participant in home and community contexts in order to familiarize my-self with their multiple literacy and spiritual practices.

AFRICAN AMERICAN SPIRITUALITIES

African American spiritualities are venues that African American people use to make meaning of contexts, realities, and entities that they encounter (Williams, 1999). Although this concept has been documented as being shared by many Blacks, it is essential to understand that not all Black people subscribe to an African American spirituality and that such spirituality does not exclude people who are not Black.

Within African American spiritualities, God is the beginning of all things as well as the creator and sustainer of life (Bridges, 2001). This is a spiritual concept that spans different religions, including Christianity, Islam, and Yoruba. Many African American people enact spiritual purposes throughout their lives rather than in compartmentalized segments (Wade-Gayles, 1995). Although African American spiritualities are complex texts with various interpretations, I focus on three tenets: (1) God as a member of the family, (2) transformative sacredness, and (3) transformation for liberation (Stewart, 1997). In their essence, these spiritualities have been defined as activist-oriented worldviews that counter interlocking systems of oppression (Martin, 2000).

Within this formulation, God stands as the most prominent family member with whom one communicates (Bridges, 2001). This framework shapes how Blacks metaphorically and physically understand the intricate relationships that they have with God as a family member (Stewart, 1997). On the one hand, God, as the head of their family, is obligated to care for them, protect them, provide resources, and guide them. On the other hand, as children of God, they are required to listen, follow moral codes, honor God as their mother/father, and live a life that illuminates God's will.

Blacks enact their spiritual literacy practices by reading and writing themselves as sacred texts, enacting the tenet of transformative sacredness. As God's children, they must redefine their self-worth, call upon their relationship with God, and harness the resources provided by the head of their family (Williams, 1999). Reading and writing one's self as a sacred text invariably entails centering one's life upon God and affirming one's sacred existence regardless of one's current situation. This tenet of transformative sacredness argues for the conscious affirmation of Blacks naming themselves as God's people and affirming their God selves by using the language tools of God talk, divine references, and visible adulation (Stewart, 1997).

The tenet of transformation for liberation is defined in the way in which spiritualities foster agency rather than subjugation, by countering oppression and creating more socially just practices (Cone, 1997; Mitchem, 2002). Blacks have drawn on their spirituality to change the conditions that shape their realities. In many cases, spiritual Blacks have translated language and systems of power that were created to enslave them into tools of liberation and visions of power (Stewart, 1997). Spiritual people understand that transformation for liberation does not always provide an immediate answer, a successful endeavor, or an end to oppression; it is a tool that enhances survival, improves quality of life, and sustains future generations.

GABE'S, KEVIN'S, AND JOSEPH'S SPIRITUALITIES

Gabe was a spiritual boy who did not align himself with any religion. Gabe defined himself as connected to the (un)seen force of God. Gabe prayed to God occasionally, spoke with God often, and believed that God was an important force in his life. He also believed that God created all the people in the world. Additionally, Gabe was connected to the (un)seen forces of his (non)living brother and father. He believed that although they had both left this earth in physical form, they were still alive in spirit, and that he had seen and communicated with his brother.

Like Gabe, Joseph and Kevin believed in an (un)seen force, called God. However, Kevin and Joseph's beliefs were grounded in the Christian religion; they envisioned God as a male god, otherwise known as Jesus. Joseph and Kevin attended church at least three times a week, played instruments during church services, and prayed daily. Kevin knew many Bible stories and verses, and often reflected on God's will. Joseph shared these characteristics, but he was more verbal and overt about his willingness to serve God and to name himself as a Christian and one of God's children. Joseph preached mini sermons, offered advice by citing God's words, and reminded people, particularly his cousin/brother Kevin, about behaviors that aligned or misaligned with God.

Naming God as Part of Your Family

The children named God as a member of their family. In Kevin's and Joseph's family-involvement collages, they included words and phrases from magazines: "God is still working on me," and "can't get enough of the master." In Kevin's collage elicitation interview, he pronounced,

"Families are good because God is part of your family." This naming also arose in one of Gabe's interviews, when he said:

> Some kids do know about God. Some kids' mothers tell them about God and some kids' mothers don't speak to them about God. My mother has talked to me about God she said he made us and when our moms have us she will be okay. . . . They don't know God made them. God made their ancestors. That's all.

In addition to naming God as a member of their family, they joined other spiritual Blacks by identifying God as seeing everything. During an interview, Gabe explained, "God sees everything. He sees us and we can't see him." Joseph later expressed this sentiment in a focus group: "You act like you don't have manners. God is going to see you. . . . I cannot run away and act like my God can't see." Gabe and Kevin echoed his words, "Yup" and "Uh-huh." In these articulations, the boys' spiritual literacy practices read and wrote God as a text who was present and visible throughout their lives, while reading and writing themselves as texts that must be responsible and accountable to God.

Drawing on God's Strength

I can feel the spirit calling
I can feel it
Inside of me

One Saturday Kevin and Rhonda were singing this verse and clapping their hands. As they sang, their mother/aunt was heard stating, "Sing well. Sing well." This prompting to the children was a spiritual literacy practice. She was encouraging them to praise God at their highest level and to recognize the power of God within them. The content of this song, the practice of singing, and the encouragement of the singing by a family members mark this song as a touchstone text. Family members enact spiritual literacy practices and in turn shape the children's own practices. These actions align with the tenet of transformative sacredness. Music identifies one's self in relation to God, as a catalyst for sustenance and a calming resource (Bridges, 2001).

Gabe continually read and wrote himself as a spiritual text that was able to call upon God's resources (Norton, 2009). In addition to communicating with God through prayer and conversation, Gabe's spiritual literacy practices entailed drawing upon his mother's words while interpreting things for himself. He clearly noted differences between his mother's and his own spiritualities, including the way that he prayed and his mother did not pray at this time in her life. He explained that he thought the death of his father and brother had something to do with the fact that his mom no longer prayed to God. Despite these differences, Gabe read and wrote his mother as strong and pondered the messages about God she offered.

> Like when my sister wanted to switch schools. My mother said school is not fun or a place to have friends. School is the place where you learn. She said that she could say her prayers to help her focus and remember that. She told me something like that too. This year, I didn't really like my new teacher. She yells too much. I started crying on the morning for school. I didn't really want to be there. . . . My mom reminded me I didn't need to like school and that there were many things I won't like in life. She tells me that God can help me get through it. She says God makes me strong and that I am strong enough to handle whatever comes my way. I always remember this.

Gabe drew on the resources of God and God's strength to help him deal with an unpleasant school experience. If we begin with the tenet of transformative sacredness, we witness the ways Gabe pondered his struggles, in dialogue with himself as God's child. Through this, he became strong enough to deal with switching schools, growing accustomed to a new teacher, and other unfortunate life circumstances. Gabe acknowledged that God would help him when he was not on solid ground (Norton, 2006).

His mother's words echoed the sentiment shared by many spiritual Blacks: that God will give you the vision to see new survival resources (Williams, 1999).

> My mother gives me the advice to call on God a lot. She says we are Black/Latino and that we have many strikes against us. The other morning she was talking to my sister and telling her that she needed a strong education because being Black/Latina and female that she had strikes against her. Plus, because she is large, she has more strikes against her. She reminded her that God can help you through. You don't need no friends; you have God. She told me to stop crying in school because then people think you are a punk and they will bother you. She told me to be strong and to stop crying—life wasn't that bad.

Unpacking these words illuminates the ways in which Gabe's mother recognized interlocking systems of oppression of race, sex, and size, all through the tenet of transformation for liberation. She sought to give her children the strategies to transform other systems of power into situations that worked for them. Gabe found these viable lessons. Throughout my research, Gabe called upon the strength of God in himself and used his spiritual literacy practices when he challenged other people who isolated him because of his stuttering, and spoke up for himself when people treated him in oppressive ways (Norton, 2009).

Kevin named God's strength as a resource during a collaborative conversation when children were asked to sculpt clay to represent their spiritualities.

> *Nadjwa*: You have two things, water and an angel. What else are
>   you going to make?
> *Kevin*: Power.
> *Nadjwa*: Power? How are you going to shape that? What is it
>   going to look like?
> *Kevin*: Like shoom! [*moves with hands*]
> *Nadjwa*: Like fish or a hand?
> *Kevin*: No power!!! [*moves hands again*] Like this.
> *Nadjwa*: Okay, so you are going to make it a flat streak.

Kevin named himself as strong, not just in the physical utterance of the words, but also in the tone, volume, certainty, and even his exasperation at my confusion. When Kevin moved his hand across the table, he moved his body and marked the affirmation of himself as God's child, a strong man with the power of God. His words echoed the sentiments in his family's literacies: proclaiming his strength, asserting the power of God, and boldly identifying as a Christian.

When we later picked us this conversation, I gained further insight.

> *Nadjwa*: What kind of power were you talking about?
> *Kevin*: I have the power to save kids from the devil . . . strength to
>   get my power and kill the devil!!
> *Joseph*: You rebuke him.
> *Nadjwa*: When you rebuke the devil, what do you do?
> *Joseph*: You have to say God's word. I rebuke him in Jesus name
>   and then you resist him and he is dead. He can't touch you. If
>   you touch him you will act like him. If you don't touch him
>   you will not act like him. . . . I just say I rebuke him in Jesus
>   name. I am a strong man and I have strength.

Kevin noted that he was strong enough to get his power, the power of God from within, in order to accomplish these feats. Kevin's words reflect Black spiritualities that shape people to read and write themselves as divine texts who can never be fully depleted from their divine energy as long as they consciously retain their connection to God (Stewart, 1997).

Joseph also asserted his voice and made himself visible as a strong man of God who used his strength to rebuke the devil by calling on God's word, by not touching the devil, and by reiterating, "I am a strong man and I have strength." When Joseph spoke, he called upon the spiritual resources to challenge people and contexts that sought to bind and enslave him (Stewart, 1997). His actions aligned with spiritual Blacks who reaffirm their "God-selves" and constantly re-ingrain within themselves their worthiness in God, which, in turn, acts as a shield so that the adversaries of God cannot harm them. Of particular importance is the way in which Joseph read and wrote himself as an agentic text with multiple strategies. Such strategies are believed to catalyze the Word of God into becoming flesh and dwelling within people as the living spirit and the power that people can apply to ensure their survival (Cannon, 1996).

Reading and Writing the "Strong Pastor Text"

Spiritual people read and write people, including their spiritual leaders, as strong texts. Kevin and Joseph both demonstrated the abilities to (1) read and write the pastor as a strong person of God, (2) read other people as pastors, and (3) draw resources from the pastor as a text in order to manifest agencies in oppressive situations.

During an interview, Kevin created a design with wood pieces, depicting a pastor and people in a church. When asked to explain it, he stated:

> People come to church and the pastor preaches to them and teaches them. They listen because the pastor is smart and helps you. The pastor reads to you out of the Bible. Our pastor comes over on the weekend. We go to his house. He cuts our hair and lets us play his car-racing video game.

Kevin's spiritual literacies included reading and writing the pastor as smart and capable of teaching other people, preaching the word of God, and helping people. The intimate relationship Kevin and Joseph had with their pastor enhanced their reading of him as a text. This is significant as we consider how Kevin, for example, began to read and write other children as a pastor. During one of our collaborative conversations when we were choosing books to make the classroom library reflect multicultural issues, Kevin articulated his thoughts.

Nadjwa: If we pick books that they like and help them to read
    better, what do you think that might help them to do?
Kevin: Make them be a preacher.
Nadjwa: A teacher? [Kevin shakes his head no.] A preacher?
Kevin: A minister.
Nadjwa: Who wants to be a minister? You?
Kevin: Just like smart people. Jorge could be a pastor [throws
    hands up]. And Christina.
Nadjwa: Why do you think they will make a good minister?
Kevin: Ministers have to know a lot, help people, and be nice.
    When the people come to church and the pastor preaches to
    them and teaches them stuff. They listen because the pastor is
    smart and helps you. The pastor reads to you out of the Bible.

Here, Kevin drew from his familial contexts and read multiple texts through spiritual lenses. He read and wrote two classmates, Jorge and Christina, as future pastor texts. He believed that these children had the potential to become pastors because they were smart, helped others, and were nice.

The importance of reading and writing the pastor and the pastor as strong person of God, who inspires God's children to find courage and strength in the face of adversity, has a central role in Black spiritualities (Cone, 1997). Moreover, Joseph read and wrote the pastor as a strong agent who was capable in times of trouble. During a focus group discussion about how families help you fight against racism, Joseph further articulated the ways in which he read and wrote the pastor as a strong man of God.

If somebody says that you are Black you are not supposed to listen to them. . . . You are supposed to say I am a pastor. A pastor
is very strong. They can do many things. They can see things that
are going to be bad. You can tell them I am strong. I am a man of
God. I am a woman of God. . . . You just say I rebuke this woman
and you can go to the church and to the pulpit. The pulpit will
help you and tell you things.

Although Joseph begins by telling a story related to challenging racist people, he transitions to offer future wisdom and strategies, enacting a liberatory praxis. In so doing, Joseph read and wrote himself and the rest of us in the focus group through the tenet of transformative sacredness. Attempting to redefine our self-worth and to call on the power of God, he explained that God provides resources in times of trouble. He read and wrote the constructs of pulpit, pastor, and God's strength as powerful resources. Joseph understood and tried to convey to us that God's power and transcendence flow through relationships between people and the pastor, who is indirectly related to God, and between people and God, as well as people and the pulpit, a sanctuary for God (Stewart, 1997).

POSSIBILITIES FOR YOUR CLASSROOM, SCHOOL, AND COMMUNITY

Inequities persist as spiritual literacies are silenced and ostracized within schools. Opening spaces to hear children such as Joseph, Kevin, and Gabe will foster greater understandings around the intersections of sociocultural theories, family literacies, and spiritualities. Moreover, although Gabe, Kevin, and Joseph had distinct but overlapping spiritualities, we can become more aware of the heterogeneity in spiritual literacy practices. By listening to children, we may reconceptualize past understandings and expand our knowledges concerning the types of texts that they see, hear, speak, listen to, and create. And although not every child engages spiritual literacies, to understand the resources in those who do, it is necessary to draw from an extended knowledge base when interacting with all children and families.

Educators and researchers need to carve out spaces where they begin to systematically investigate the range of spiritual literacies practices that exist within diverse contexts. This may entail asking more questions, observing families' expansive literacies practices, spending time in diverse communities, and devising research endeavors that directly investigate these ideas. In order to do this, people must first name spiritualities as an aspect of culture and second recognize the value of spiritualities within many communities.

Currently, the field of family literacies does not have deepened understandings about spiritual literacies practices. This, in turn, shapes the ways in which educators and researchers are (not) able to construct supportive structures for spiritual people. Without accurate understandings of lesser known spiritualities or surface understandings of spiritual literacies practices, teachers inaccurately use language to talk about, label, identify, and construct people. For example, children who believe they can read the energy in other people and then distance themselves from particular types of energies, may be read as antisocial, friendless, or weird. Without understanding these spiritual literacies practices, teachers may misdiagnose, inaccurately group, or falsely misconstrue a child's actions.

Greater effort must be made to create spaces for families and children who engage spiritual literacies to do so without the constant need to censor, hide, and assimilate these practices. More facility is needed to understand the ways in which people read and write themselves and others as spiritual texts and the ways in which these literacies inform actions. We must advocate for valuing spiritual literacies, selecting texts that foster these literacies, and making them visible in culturally responsive pedagogies. Without such efforts, we will continue to fall short and privilege particular literacies at the expense of spiritual people like Gabe, Kevin, and Joseph who name spiritual literacy practices as imperative parts of their lives.

REFERENCES

Bridges, F. W. (2001). *Resurrection song: African American spirituality*. Maryknoll, NY: Orbis Books.

Cannon, K. (1996). *Katie's canon*. New York: Continuum.

Cone, J. (1997). *God of the oppressed*. New York: Orbis Books.

Freire, P. (1998). *Pedagogy of the oppressed* (rev. ed.). New York: Continuum.

Freire, P., & Macedo, D. (1987). *Literacy: Reading the word and the world*. Westport, CT: Bergin & Garvey.

Gallego, M., & Hollingsworth, S. (Eds.). (2000). *What counts as literacy: Challenging the school standard*. New York: Teachers College Press.

Hull, A. G. (Ed.). (2001). *Soul talk: The new spirituality of African American women*. Rochester, VT: Inner Traditions International.

Lewis, C., Enciso, P., & Moje, E. (Eds.). (2007). *Reframing sociocultural research on literacy: Identity, agency, and power*. Mahwah, NJ: Erlbaum.

Martin, J. (2000). *More than chains and toil: A Christian work ethic of enslaved women*. Louisville, KY: Westminster John Knox Press.

Mitchem, S. (2002). *Introducing womanist theology*. New York: Orbis Books.

Norton, N. (2005). Permitanme hablar: Allow me to speak. *Language Arts, 83*(2), 118–127.

Norton, N. (2006). Talking spirituality with family members: Black and Latina/o children co-researcher methodologies. *Urban Review, 38*(4), 313–334.

Norton, N. (2009). Negotiating speech-related disabilities and interpersonal school structures with agencies and intersecting identities. *Disabilities Studies Quarterly, 29*(3).

Stewart, C. F., III. (1997). *Soul survivors: An African American spirituality*. Louisville, KY: Westminster John Knox Press.

Wade-Gayles, G. (Ed.). (1995). *My soul is a witness: African-American women's spirituality*. Boston: Beacon Press.

Williams, D. (1999). *Sisters in the wilderness*. New York: Orbis Books.

A RESPONSE TO CHAPTER 8

Stuart Greene

Nadjwa Norton's chapter brings together a number of central themes raised by others in this section: (a) the children's immersion in culturally relevant literate practices at home; (b) the ways children use literacy as a form of agency in their everyday lives; (c) the gap between the rich home literate experiences of children and the often inauthentic reading and writing experiences children encounter at school; (d) the difficulties that children have attaching meaning to school when their experiences are not included in classroom activities; and (e) the ways in which classroom experiences can silence students.

As a result of silencing, children create what some might call a third space where they are able to forge relationships with peers who share a similar sense of community, identity, and well-being. The portraits of Joseph, Kevin, and Gabe remind us of the funds of knowledge that students bring to classrooms and the reasons why educators must find ways to create spaces in classrooms where students feel comfortable expressing themselves, even in the face of difference. Such a classroom would be what Mary Louis Pratt (1991) has called a contact zone—where students are able to raise issues that they find meaningful in a context of exploring diverse opinions and where their ideas are given legitimacy.

However, Ryan's and Norton's chapters underscore a puzzle that teachers must negotiate continually: the ways in which open discussions about family, sexuality, and faith affect students. It is difficult for teachers and students to confront differences that make them uncomfortable. Then again, the spaces teachers open to reinforce children's sense of identity can easily silence students who do not share the same values. And this problem is even more acute in public schools where laws prohibit discussion of faith.

Each chapter in Part II makes visible beliefs, values, and histories that are often invisible to educators. Recognizing the assumptions we bring, has the potential to enhance what we teach. This is the point of the chapter that follows. Rosario Ordoñez-Jasis and Susana Flores describe ways to bridge home and school by sharing families' literacy autobiographies with teachers. Doing so helps teachers examine their assumptions about how literacy develops in the context of culture, ethnicity, history, language, and geography.

REFERENCE

Pratt, M. L. (1991). *Profession 91*. New York: MLA, 33–40.

CHAPTER 9

DESCUBRIENDO HISTORIAS/ UNCOVERING STORIES

The Literacy Worlds of Latino Children and Families

Rosario Ordoñez-Jasis
Susana Y. Flores

This chapter investigates the journey of four early childhood educators and two researcher/educators who embarked on an inquiry-based project in the neighborhood where most of them were raised. They sought to capture and capitalize on family literacy practices found in their dynamic, ever-changing, mostly Latino bilingual and bicultural school community. This collective journey gave the teachers the tools to critically reflect upon how this "new" community knowledge could be incorporated into their early childhood education program's literacy curriculum.

Through reflection and dialogue, these teachers also gained a better understanding of how the life histories of the parents—specifically their literacy autobiographies—were culturally, socially, and historically congruent with the literacy practices that shaped them personally and professionally. Moreover, the new understandings they gained about the richness of diverse family literacy practices led them to critically question the dominant discourse about what constitutes literacy development in young bicultural children. At a time when much of the research has focused on the cultural incongruities between homes and schools, the teachers in this project—through their ethnographic work with families and households—offer deeper understandings of how the literacy-rich resources of a community can help educators gain knowledge that can be used to build potential literacy bridges between diverse homes and schools.

COMPLICATING COMMONSENSE VIEWS OF PARENTS AND COMMUNITIES

As described in the introduction to this volume, Moll and González (2004) identified rich "funds of knowledge" possessed by Latino families. Their work, and the work of other researchers (Gadsden, 2000; Garcia, Jensen, & Cuellar, 2006), highlights literacy gains made by young children in classrooms with culturally knowledgeable teachers. Unfortunately, for many students, a skills-based, English-only prescriptive curriculum often privileges schooled literacy over out-of-school home literacy practices.

Many studies have sought to uncover the cultural and linguistic negotiations enacted by teachers and families from different backgrounds (Au, 2009; Heath, 1983), but fewer studies have examined the dynamics involved when teachers and families share the same cultural, social, historical, and linguistic background. Darder (1991) offers an important reminder that a mere sharing of the same cultural heritage or primary language is not in itself a guarantee that the cultural and linguistic values and dispositions of students and families will be incorporated or legitimated within the sphere of the classroom. Darder argues that educators also must encompass a spirit of solidarity with the families of their students, or develop the Freirian notion of "ideological clarity" (Freire, 1994), which "affirms the right of individuals to be educated in their own language and learning style and the right to maintain a bicultural identity" (Darder, 1991, p. 119). We believe that the voices and perspectives presented in this chapter will expand the conversation among all educators regarding relevant literacy practices within Latino households.

A NOTE ON METHODS

This project reports on the ethnographic work of four Latina teachers and two Latina university researcher/educators over a 6-month period in a Latino working-class school district in southern California. The preschool educators wanted to find ways to actively and intentionally connect the practices of the home with school-related goals and objectives in the area of early literacy development.

Each teacher and researcher conducted in-depth, open-ended interviews with five Latino families from their classrooms. Interviewers asked four broad questions: What is literacy to you? What were your childhood experiences with literacy at home and in school? What literacy practices do you engage in now? What literacy practices do you engage in with your child? After the interviews had been conducted, the teachers and university researchers co-analyzed the data, adopting Delgado-Bernal's (1998) notion of cultural intuition. Delgado-Bernal introduced the concept of cultural intuition to describe the unique insights that many Chicana/Latina educators bring to their research, based on their social, cultural, political, and professional histories.

We believe this concept of cultural intuition applies to the ethnographic work of the Latina teachers and informs their everyday interactions with Latino families in their schools. This cultural intuition also incorporates the personal and collective experiences of the Latina university researchers—one was raised in this community and the other in a neighboring city—and allows for more critical understanding of the forces that impact the literacy lives of the teachers and families in this project. All six women interacted with families as common stakeholders, with familiarity and ease. Processes of learning and knowing are situated from living within a particular community (Darder, 1991). The Latina educators shared a deeper understanding of the parents' lived realities, and thus the families' narratives were better interpreted and represented.

The Teachers

The four teacher-participants included Ms. Brunie, Ms. Patty, Ms. Maggie, and Ms. Letty. Ms. Brunie is a veteran preschool teacher and self-described "champion" of bilingual education. She recently was recognized for her 25 years of service to the district. Born and raised by a single mother in the United States, Brunie attended public schools in a nearby district with similar demographics. She holds a bachelor's degree from a public university. Ms. Patty also was born in the United States and attended schools in the district from preschool through her high school graduation. Ms. Patty has taught preschool for 14 years in the district, and her daughter attended elementary school there. Ms. Patty currently resides in a neighboring city and recently graduated with a bachelor's degree from a private university. Ms. Maggie has taught preschool in the district for 8 years. Born in Mexico, she and her family moved to the United States when she was 9 years old and she was raised in a neighboring community with similar demographics. Ms. Maggie is also bilingual, recently has received an AA degree from the local community college, and plans to transfer to a 4-year university. A single mother of two boys, Ms. Maggie resides in the local community, and her children attend schools in the district. Ms. Letty was born in Mexico where she was employed as a teacher. She moved to the United States with her family as a young adult. Her grown children attended schools in the district, and, as a returning student, Ms. Letty recently celebrated her graduation from a 4-year university.

The Families

Thirty families were selected to represent the wide range of demographic variables found within the heterogeneous local Latino community. Families differed according to socioeconomic status, educational level, and generational status (first generation, second generation, recent immigrant). All parents were bilingual (English and Spanish); however, the majority of parents were Spanish dominant. Although the majority of the parents were of Mexican descent, there was an active attempt to recruit parents from other Latin American countries. Eighteen mothers, ten fathers, and two grandmothers participated in the project. The interviews took place in either the families' homes or the teachers' classrooms. As Ms. Letty noted with a smile, "Everybody was excited talking about their stories!"

THE CENTRALITY OF CULTURALLY BASED HOME LITERACY ACTIVITIES

Although many educators continue to assume that poor, or linguistically diverse, homes provide little that prepares children for the school curriculum, scholars have found that Mexican-origin families indeed provide literacy-based experiences for their children, hold high expectations for their offspring, and provide warm, loving homes. Auerbach (2001), in her work with a parent-involvement literacy program, found that Latino families advocated for their children and lived in social contexts that provided many unrecognized literacy experiences. Not surprisingly, we recognized a rich oral tradition in the families we interviewed. In our analysis of parent interviews we identified key themes in the parents' literacy autobiographies, namely, the centrality of culturally based learning practices that included sharing romance stories, ghost stories, and songs.

Romancing the Story

Snow, Tabors, and Dickinson (2001) highlight the strong relationship between children's interaction with oral language and later reading abilities. Storytelling, for example, "requires participants to develop understandings beyond the here and now," as children learn to explain, describe, narrate, tell jokes, or pretend (p. 2). Furthermore, stories that are authentic, meaningful, and culturally relevant enhance children's under-standing and allow for greater connection and comprehension (Flores-Duenas, 2004). For many of the parents in this project, relating the story of how they met their spouse took on a fairytale-like quality. Ms. Patty describes her interviews in this way:

> A common thing that came up was how the parents met. The mothers would tell their children how they met their father, how they were born, and, you know, the songs that were playing when they were born. Another parent likes to tell her children how they met in the park. They were going to school and were studying in the park. They ended up getting married. They talked about how that was their child's favorite story, a romantic little story.

Another mother recounted how her children enjoyed listening to her and her husband's love story. She shared, "They like to hear stories about how my husband and I were when we were children. And how we met and fell in love. I like this sharing time with them."

These romance stories with the male and female protagonist reflected important story elements, including a beginning, a middle, a climax, and a happily ever after sentiment commonly found in children's literature. McLaren (1994) reminds us that "translating an experience into a story is perhaps the most fundamental act of human understanding" (p. 92). Indeed, through the telling and retelling of stories, families were able to construct and reconstruct meaning and order in their lives. These sto-ries served a dual purpose in strengthening cultural bonds among family members and simultaneously building essential literacy skills with their children.

Ghost Stories: *El Cucuy* and *Los Cholos*

The popularity of ghost and mystery stories transcends linguistic boundaries and literacy levels. As a genre, ghost stories are very popular in Latin America. Ghost stories in this context have the power to enter-tain but also serve as tales to both caution and educate. Many of the par-ents echoed the use of *El Cucuy* (or The Boogeyman) stories to warn their children of very real dangers. For example, one father fondly recalled his mother's storytelling bedtime rituals.

> My mom would make up fairytales. She would always tell us stories before going to bed; stories with lots of detail and action.

> Sometimes the stories were scary. She would tell me about not walking away from the house alone because *El Cucuy* would get me.

Another parent giggled as she explained about other kinds of "ghosts" and "witches" that haunted her childhood home.

> Well my father would tell us that there was a ghost in the house. He would make noises and hide our things. He would hide behind the door and jump out and say, "BOO!" He also would tease us that we belonged to an old *bruja* (witch) who lived down the street. He said that he took us in because she didn't like kids. If we didn't behave he would threaten to give us back!

For these parents, *El Cucuy* was always present, waiting to appear if children wandered too far away from home or misbehaved. Interestingly, as parents learned to contend with the new real and perceived dangers of living in an urban area, the legend of *El Cucuy* transformed into stories surrounding *Los Cholos* (gang members). In the following extended conversation from one of our meetings, we reflected on the parents' use of this type of genre:

Ms. Letty: One of the parents from here *siempre le hablaban de Los Cholos que se habian peleado y le cortaron la cabeza al senor. Y la cabeza la usaban de pelota.* (One of the parents from here would always talk about the gangsters and how they had been in a fight and they cut the man's head off and they used the head as a ball.)

Ms. Brunie: *Por eso le tienen miedo a Los Cholos.* (That is why they are afraid of the gangsters.)

Susana: That is a good *Cucuy* story in a way.

Ms. Brunie: Yeah! I had a little boy years back *que le tenia mucho miedo a Los Cholos*. He might have heard a story. (I had a little boy years back that was very afraid of the Cholos. He might have heard that story).

Ghost stories and their variations hold the power to unleash the imagination and creativity of both the storyteller and his or her audience, while affording families the opportunity to playfully tease their children in culturally appropriate ways. Sociocultural theory views families as powerful socializing agents as they introduce their children to the words and worlds of the community to which they belong (Freire, 1994). These tales and folklore served as opportunities for parents to socialize their children through language, while socializing them to use language (Morrow,

2009) in a way that reflects the cultural and linguistic worldviews of the families, and alerting them to potential dangers via cautionary tales.

Remembering Children's Songs of Love and *Alegria*

Perhaps the warmest moments are those of a parent, aunt or uncle, grandmother or grandfather singing *canciones de cuna*, or lullabies. The intimacy of the moment is made memorable by the joy of song. This sentiment was repeated to us by nearly every one of the family members we interviewed. One *abuelita* (grandmother) recalled singing to her children and grandchildren, *duermete mi nino, duermete me ya* (go to sleep my little one, go now to sleep), in a soft hushed voice as she rocked them to sleep. Others spoke of more upbeat songs with the opposite objective of energizing with joy, or *alegria*.

Parents similarly recounted moments in songs with their children that were rooted in traditional Latin American culture and also solid mainstream culture, not uncommon to the bicultural Latino experience. While one mother sang Disney tunes with her children, another mother sang *Mariachi canciones* (songs) with her children. This mother proudly shared, "*Yo canto. Canto con mariachi. Cuando practico ensayan conmigo. No canto profesional, canto familiar. En el carro cantamos. Es algo normal para ellos.*" ("I sing. I sing with mariachi. When I practice they rehearse with me. I don't sing professionally, I sing with my family. In the car we sing. It is something normal to them.")

For the Latino families who participated in our project, these songs were characterized by the unifying emotion of joy. However, there are other equally significant events at play. Lullabies, silly songs, and rhymes are but one way of transmitting culture(s) orally. The four early childhood educators already had a history of successfully engaging in practices that capitalized on culturally specific songs in support of early literacy. They recalled that these songs were in many cases the same songs that they grew up with and were central to the construction of their literacy identities. As the teachers carefully listened to the stories of the families and reflected upon the richness of literacy practices they found in the homes, a heightened consciousness soon developed as they came to rediscover and better appreciate the benefits of home-based stories and songs in the emergent literacy process. In the following excerpt from one of our data analysis meetings, Ms. Patty recalls a moment in her classroom:

> Today I heard a little boy sing, *Toda la Vida*. I thought, "Hey I like that song!" I turned around and saw that it was Zachary so I started to dance with him. When grandma got there I told her he was

singing all day. She said he sings it with his dad and that's how he knows the whole song and it goes like this, *"Toda la vida comiendo tacos en la esquina por que mi mami no cocina."* ("All my life eating tacos on the corner because my mother doesn't cook."). And I am like, "Oh my God. Oh my God, all this rhyming! *Esquina y cocina* (Corner and kitchen). Let me write this down so I can share at our meeting!"

BUILDING LITERACY BRIDGES

We found, however, that parents did not overtly connect their rich home literacy practices with traditional notions of early literacy development "support." Many of the Latino parents we interviewed clearly separated the language "play" they engaged in with their children from the more serious literacy "work" that was clearly part of the drive for "school readiness." The preschool teachers began to draw upon their own experiences to make sense of this unfolding theme. The topic of our conversations with the teachers transitioned to making clear connections among the various types of literacy practices found in homes, and how they can be better connected with school-based literacy expectations.

We discovered that almost all the parents interviewed did not learn to read until first grade and initially were surprised, even alarmed, that their children were exposed to emergent reading and writing practices at the preschool level. One parent expressed this particular sentiment by stating, "I cannot believe they are expected to know so much before kindergarten! I see that what we learned in first and second grade, they are now learning in preschool." Most of the parents reported that they learned to read in school and not at home, and that the kind of instruction they received was heavily phonics-based. Not surprisingly, when the parents were asked, "What kinds of literacy practices do you engage in with your child?" the responses suggested a heavy emphasis on phonics instruction as well. Parents mentioned that they "practiced the sounds of the alphabet," "pointed to letters of the alphabet," "used flash cards," taught "sight words" and "basic skills," "practiced sounding out words," and emphasized "neatness" with their children. We were heartened to learn that quite a few parents supported their children's biliteracy development by reading to their children, reinforcing vocabulary words, and teaching the letters of the alphabet, all in both Spanish and English. One parent supported his child's biliteracy development by making a built-in bookshelf in their living room. He very matter-of-factly explained, *"Tengo un lado para libros en espanol y otro lado para libros en ingles."* ("I have one side for books in Spanish and the other side for books in English.")

The functional and practical uses of literacy echoed throughout most of the interviews: "I work with my son in teaching him the basic skills he will need for his future schooling," while another commented, "Learning a lot of activities in school will help them to learn in the future." We also discovered that an overwhelming majority of the parents were anxious about their children's literacy development. Parents often believed that the main purpose for engaging children in "literacy" activities was to prepare them for kindergarten. Despite reassurance from her child's teacher, one mother described her apprehension.

> I feel bad that I sometimes push my son to learn with flashcards. He doesn't like it. I know and we both get frustrated, but I heard he will need to take a test even before he walks through the kindergarten doors!

Unlike stories and songs, few parents described these literacy experiences as "enjoyable" or "fun." The majority of the parents differentiated between the "serious" work involved in developing children's early literacy abilities and the positive playfulness and bonding associated with stories, singing, and everyday conversations.

The following conversational excerpts exemplify how, through reflection and dialogue, the teachers intuitively drew upon their own literacy memories as a starting point for interrogating prevailing assumptions about what constitutes as legitimate literacy practices. Specifically, we began to rethink the centrality of schools in this process and the role teachers have in reshaping parents' understandings of biliteracy development.

> *Ms. Patty:* You know I felt like many of [the parents] thought literacy was just repeating the alphabet and pointing out letters. Only one of them mentioned having a conversation or playing pretend as part of literacy. This message they get from schools.
>
> *Ms. Letty:* I learned that parents help [their children] in different ways but they don't think they are helping their children in literacy development when they are talking, singing, or telling them stories.
>
> *Ms. Maggie:* [My mom] never went to school and she never read a book to us but she told us "La Llorona" ("The Wailing

Woman"). . . . We used to pretend that she would take us on
a picnic . . . and she would create stories about our animals,
the dogs, chickens, and roosters. She used to say, "Get
everything ready, tomorrow we are going to have a picnic in
the park." We would be all happy and excited. The next day
she said, *"Andale, los sanwiches mi hijos por que nos vamos a ir."*
("Hurry, get the sandwiches because we're going to go.") We
are going to pretend that we are going to the park." So we
would go through the front door and walk two times around
the house.

Ms. Letty: Parents need our help extending what they are already
doing with literacy. They are doing a lot. But we need to give
them that message better.

Although the teachers had all adopted a culturally/linguistically responsive and balanced literacy curriculum, the practice of conducting open-
ended interviews with the parents allowed them to come to new understandings. They became aware that explicit, skills-based literacy activities
were unintentionally privileged over culturally relevant and less formal-
ized literacy activities. The teachers committed themselves to centralize
the songs, ghost and love stories, pretend play, and rhyme that families
engaged in with pure enjoyment, passion, and pride.

The teachers also began to seriously question dominant statewide
assumptions about the direction of school readiness and mainstream
preschool curricula. Moreover, they started to rethink the importance
of culturally and socially relevant family literacy interactions in further-
ing the goals and objectives of not only their language arts program,
but other aspects of their developmentally appropriate curriculum. For
example, in the extended conversation described above, social pretend
play between Ms. Maggie and her mother had a role not only in her early literacy development, but in developing "symbolic transformations of
the real world" (Katz, 2001, p. 56). This interactive and interpersonal
"dramatic play" allowed Ms. Maggie's mother to expose her children to
elements of their culture—via contextualized "oral storytelling" about
the ranch chickens and other animals at "the park" and decontextual-
ized folklore of *La Llorona*—while engaging them in imaginative alternatives to real-life scenarios. Most important, these kinds of culturally
contextualized oral storytelling and pretend play scenarios that occur
within Latino households on an everyday basis allow children to learn
to read their worlds in new and exciting ways (Ada & Zubizarreta, 2001;
Freire, 1994).

POSSIBILITIES FOR YOUR CLASSROOM, SCHOOL, AND COMMUNITY

As I interviewed the families, I got totally different insight from each parent I talked to. It was good! I understand how the past relates to the present. The parents' own childhood experiences with literacy matches where they are now—how they see literacy, what they expect for their kids. I was able to connect to so much of what they said!
                                                                              —Ms. Brunie

The literacy autobiographies and other stories collected as part of this project highlight the power of teacher inquiry as a means to learn from, and connect to, the literacy-based pedagogies and practices of diverse families. The four Latina teachers in this study suggest ways that early childhood educators can go about establishing literacy partnerships with Latino parents on behalf of children's early biliteracy development.

Student Literacy Portfolios

Early childhood educators should foster authentic parent–teacher literacy partnerships where respectful, reciprocal, and horizontal relationships are developed. The teachers in the study agreed that parents and other caregivers are important sources of untapped cultural and linguistic knowledge. Information gained about families' socially and culturally relevant literacy practices can help educators build essential "literacy portfolios" for their students. Literacy questionnaires are powerful tools that allow teachers to uncover stories among families within their own classrooms so they are better able to understand literacy in the life of their students outside the classroom walls. Teachers can ask parents or other caregivers the following five open-ended questions as they begin to build a literacy portfolio for each class member:

1. What is the primary language of your home?
2. What kinds of literacy practices do you engage in with your child(ren)? In what language?
3. What kinds of literacy activities do you enjoy?
4. What would you like to tell me about your child(ren) and their literacy development?
5. What are your goals and expectations for your child(ren)?

As the stories of the parents in this study revealed, the power and potential of their literacy-rich daily interactions with their children were, for the most part, unrealized and not viewed as "literacy activities." Influenced by their own literacy education as well as the current push in California schools for heavy phonics-based literacy instruction, many parents, instead, had internalized a skills-based view of what constitutes early literacy parental support. Therefore, it is important for teachers to explore with families a broadened definition of literacy so parents are able more readily to recognize the "nontraditional" ways they support their children's early literacy development.

Community Literacy Mapping

Schools are located in dynamic, ever-changing communities with both historical records and contemporary resources that can help early childhood educators understand students and their families better. Community literacy mapping is an inquiry-based method that promotes increased interactions among teachers and families by removing potential cultural barriers and unearthing cultural and linguistic assets. "Mapping" the community surrounding the school—by taking photos, observing the neighborhood, taking notes, and interacting with the people who work and live in the area—should allow teachers to "see" the literacy needs and resources of the community with new lenses. It also can help teachers gain knowledge about the depth and diversity of the literacy practices of members of their school community. Specifically, community literacy mapping will enable teachers to:

1. Identify and interact with the literacy organizations that exist within the community,
2. Uncover possible literacy needs in the community,
3. Locate different kinds of formal/informal businesses in the community that have the potential to partner in literacy endeavors or initiatives,
4. Identify formal and informal gathering places where families may engage in literacy practices, and
5. Discover specific and important cultural or linguistic events and their meanings in local contexts.

The overall goal for teachers is to understand how this community knowledge can be incorporated into their curriculum, their interactions with families, or family literacy programs/workshops, as described below.

Bilingual and Biliterate Family Literacy Workshops: Building Bridges

Conducting bilingual family literacy workshops is a mutually beneficial way to build literacy bridges between schools and homes. Incorporating information gathered from student literacy portfolios and community literacy mapping, teachers can invite members from the community—librarians, curators, writers, illustrators, poets, community leaders, local business owners and service providers—to serve as guest speakers at family literacy workshops. Community members can narrate stories, sing songs, share their oral traditions, or conduct read-alouds with culturally relevant children's books. Within these events the teachers' role is key in helping parents make the critical link between the sponsored literacy event and the essential literacy elements they can foster in young children. Building these literacy bridges validates the pedagogies of the home and community while connecting families to the school's language arts curriculum. Examples of such bridges include young children's heightened awareness of the rhythm, rhyme, and other linguistic structures of the home language via songs and poetry in the primary language; the enhancement of abstract thought, imagination, and listening skills during oral storytelling; the development of key vocabulary and other important story elements as guest speakers describe their oral traditions; and the connection to text that occurs when children are exposed to quality literature that mirrors their words and worlds.

The teachers who participated in this project—already skilled at providing students with opportunities for active engagement in an array of culturally and linguistically responsive literacy activities—learned to draw upon their own literacy recollections in order to reaffirm their commitment to validate the multitude of literacy-based daily pedagogies found in homes. However, all four early childhood educators agreed that teachers need time to collaborate with their peers in professional learning communities in order to share their successes, challenges, hopes, and fears as they work toward these goals. Nurturing such inclusive family literacy practices is not only necessary to build important literacy bridges with diverse families but an essential element of a culturally/linguistically responsive, balanced, and developmentally appropriate early literacy program.

Author's Note: We would like to express our most sincere gratitude and appreciation to "las maestras"—Brunie, Letty, Maggie, and Patty—for their contributions to this project. We also recognize the School Readiness Initiative preschool teachers for their dedication and commitment to the literacy lives of their students.

REFERENCES

Ada, A., & Zubizarreta, R. (2001). Parent narratives: The cultural bridge between Latino parents and their children. In M. de la Luz & J. Halcon (Eds.), *The best for our children: Critical perspectives on literacy for Latino students* (pp. 55–67). New York: Teachers College Press.

Au, K. (2009). A multicultural perspective on policies for improving literacy achievement: Equity and excellence. In M. L. Kamil, P. D. Pearson, & R. Barr (Eds.), *Handbook of reading research* (Vol. III, pp. 835–852). Mahwah, NJ: Earlbaum.

Auerbach, E. (2001). Considering the multiliteracies pedagogy: Looking through the lens of family literacy. In M. Kalantzis & B. Cope (Eds.), *Transformation in language and literacy: Perspectives on multiliteracies* (pp. 99–112). Victoria, Australia: Common Ground.

Darder, A. (1991). *Culture and power in the classroom: A critical foundation for bicultural education.* Westport, CT: Bergin & Garvey.

Delgado-Bernal, D. (1998). Using a Chicana feminist epistemology in educational research. *Harvard Educational Review, 68*(4), 555–582.

Flores-Duenas, L. (2004). Reader response, culturally familiar literature, and reading comprehension. In F. Boyd & C. Brook (Eds.), *Multicultural and multilingual literacy and language. Contexts and practices* (pp. 180–205). New York: Guilford Press.

Freire, P. (1994). *Pedagogy of hope: Reliving pedagogy of the oppressed.* New York: Continuum.

Gadsden, V. (2000). Intergenerational literacy within families. *Handbook of the National Reading Conference Yearbook, 43*, 871–887.

Garcia, E., Jensen, B., & Cuellar, D. (2006). Early academic achievement of Hispanics in the U.S.: Implications for teacher preparation. *The New Educator, 2*(2), 123–147.

Heath, S. B. (1983). *Ways with words: Language, life, and work in communities and classrooms.* Cambridge: Cambridge University Press.

Katz, J. (2001). Playing at home: The talk of pretend play. In D. Dickinson & P. Tabors (Eds.), *Beginning literacy with language: Young children learning at home and school* (pp. 53–73). Baltimore: Paul H. Brookes.

McLaren, A. (1994). *The Chinese femme fatale: Stories from the Ming period.* Broadway, Australia: Wild Peony.

Moll, L., & Gonzalez, N. (2004). Beginning where children are. In O. Santa Ana (Ed.), *Tongue-tied: The lives of multilingual children in public education* (pp. 45–61). Lanham, MD: Rowman & Littlefield.

Morrow, L. (2009). *Literacy development in the early years: Helping children read and write.* Boston: Pearson.

Snow, C., Tabors, P., & Dickinson, D. (2001). Language development in the early years. In D. Dickinson & P. Tabors (Eds.), *Beginning literacy with language: Young children learning at home and school* (pp. 1–25). Baltimore: Paul H. Brookes.

A RESPONSE TO CHAPTER 9

Stuart Greene

Rosario Ordoñez-Jasis and Susana Flores offer insight into the family literacies of Mexican immigrant parents who impart *educacion* to their children through a rich tradition of language and history. But the literacy practices that children experience at home and that permeate their communities, are often absent in school. Not until the teachers read the families' literacy autobiographies did they fully appreciate the breadth of the children's literacy repertoires and experiences. The implication for Ordoñez-Jasis and Flores is that teacher education programs should include a sustained focus on family literacy as a means for encouraging partnerships between teachers and parents. The lessons teachers and parents provide children can be mutually informing.

At the same time, the authors also offer a word of caution—that merely sharing cultural and linguistic practices will not ensure that teachers will respect and give legitimacy to students' literacies. Equally important, Valdés (1996) argues that educators must resist simple definitions of culture and recognize the beliefs and values embedded in the structure of immigrant families. Although she wrote her ethnographic study over 15 years ago, Valdés's observations are relevant today.

> In this age, when there is talk about the value of diversity, both practitioners and policymakers must be willing to accept the fact that new immigrants bring with them models of living successfully that can not only enrich our society but can also provide protection for these new Americans in what is now a very dangerous new world. (p. 203)

In the end, we are left with one final thought that sums up what others in this volume have tried to express—that difference does not equal deficit. As educators, we cannot fix the problem of underachievement by changing parents through well-intentioned interventions. Instead, we must reevaluate our own beliefs and assumptions in ways that lead to greater openness about what it means to be literate.

REFERENCE

Valdés, G. (1996). Con respeto: *Bridging the distances between culturally diverse families and schools.* New York: Teachers College Press.

CONNECTING PARENT INVOLVEMENT AND FAMILY LITERACY

Stuart Greene
Catherine Compton-Lilly

The chapters in this edited volume complicate commonsense and traditional notions of parent involvement, and provide counternarratives to deficit views of families.

This requires listening to parents' stories, recognizing the resources they bring, respecting nonconventional forms of involvement and unconventional literacy practices, and revealing and supporting acts of agency and community activism. These accounts of parents draw our attention to forces in schooling and society that foster or impede parent involvement.

By highlighting the perspectives of parents relative to schooling and literacy, we draw attention to local contexts and highlight local issues, practices, relationships, needs, and literacies. Yet local spaces bring social histories that children and parents must negotiate as they move in and out of multiple spaces, including homes, schools, and communities. To address these issues, we turn our attention to "place-conscious" education (Gruenewald, 2005).

PLACE-CONSCIOUS EDUCATION

In developing a conception of place-conscious education, Gruenewald (2005) suggests that we cannot take physical spaces like school for granted or ignore the historical, cultural, and ideological processes that have shaped them. Schools exist as the result of purposeful decisions and choices that people have made to advance the goals of our society's economic, moral, and political well-being. However, some citizens have been invited to participate in decision-making processes while others have not. Thus not all people view schools in the same way. For some, schools can be nurturing places that foster upward mobility; for others, they can be sites of conflict where the playing field is never equal. This is why parents often can teach us perspectives that may challenge our worldviews and assumptions.

Space, especially as conceptualized by some critical geographers (Harvey, 2006) and educators (Lipman, 2007), addresses how schools can both enable and impede parents' presence there. Traditionally, parental presence at school has been a key marker of parent involvement. However, attendance at school is inextricably linked to how ideology, economics, and power shape relationships within local contexts. For the past 20 years, we have seen a mix of low economic growth and increasing discrepancies between rich and poor, unemployment, and an assault on organized labor (Harvey, 2006, 2007). Indeed, school policy is inextricably tied to a highly stratified labor force, gentrification, and displacement of low-paid workers, particularly in communities of color.

More often than not, parents are excluded from making school policies. Parents are not invited discuss policy decisions, nor do they associate the activities that occur at school with their everyday lives. This isolation from school policy development is especially problematic when school decisions have significant effects on children's lives (e.g., policies related to standards and to testing). However, all children are held to the standards that are accepted by schools, and failure to achieve these educational goals can threaten economic well-being, security, stable employment, and home life, reinforcing a sense of difference, marginalization, and disenfranchisement.

As we develop theories, we need to ground our understandings in the everyday lives of families. What significance and meanings do parents attach to school? How can we characterize the relationships that parents and teachers create within such spaces? Who determines who gets to speak? Whose stories are told and whose voices are silenced? These questions contextualize the ways in which memory, history, and identity shape how parents perceive education and literacy. School is an agent of cultural and symbolic power that has served to educate, but also has the power to exclude.

CREATING SPACES OF HOPE

The extent to which parents will feel connected to schools is a complex structural issue that educators must address if we expect parents to be partners in their children's education. The lens of critical geography brings into focus the ways in which economic policies have created a stratified society that plays out in neighborhoods and in schools. Our nation's poorest families lack economic stability, resulting in continual changes in housing and employment, and complicating the relationships that must be forged between homes and schools.

If parents are to feel more connected to schools, it is essential to unravel the complexities of the places we call schools. This entails recognizing power as being at the heart of school relationships. Unfortunately, existing hierarchies of administrators and policymakers are divorced from local conversations and the contexts in which families live. As hooks (1990) and others maintain, those living on the margins create their own spaces of hope where they can imagine alternatives to dominant economic arrangements.

By creating spaces of hope, informed by principles of social justice and the voices of parents, we can provide access to quality education, promote inclusion and fairness, address the learning needs of children, and provide equitable distributions of material and emotional resources. In turn, we offer strategies for teaching based on ethnographies of place that provide opportunities for students and teachers to explore their local communities. These strategies have the potential to connect the process of teaching and learning to classrooms and communities where teaching and learning occur. "Involvement" extends far beyond conference days, volunteering in classrooms, and field trips. Parents can be invited into all aspects of schooling.

POSSIBILITIES FOR PARENT INVOLVEMENT AND FAMILY LITERACY

Parents bring powerful networks of knowledge, beliefs, and values to educating their children. Throughout this book we have highlighted some of the ways educators can create strong partnerships with parents. This means understanding parents' identities, the structure of their families, and the range of literacies that they use in their daily lives. Specifically, we can do some of the following:

- Collect the narratives of parents to inform parent–teacher partnerships that are respectful and based on reciprocal relationships.
- Uncover the rich literacies and traditions of diverse families.
- Demonstrate that our invitations are authentic and purposeful.

- Collaborate with parents to define the significant roles they can play in schools and in their children's learning.
- Ensure that parents have the materials and information they need in order to assist children at home, participate in policy conversations, and act on behalf of children in their community.
- Design policies that engage parents in the workings of schools— hire parents as part-time helpers in classrooms, create parental advisory boards, conduct interview studies with parents in local communities.
- Recognize and challenge historical practices related to parent involvement and family literacy (e.g., parenting as women's work, privileging middle-class notions of parenting).

Forging relationships with parents also entails working with them to identify children's strengths as learners and talents. We can:

- Recognize the technological practices of children and extend these into school settings.
- Respect children's right to decide when and how to share family practices and beliefs.
- Invite students to talk about their out-of-school literacies and interests.
- Stock classrooms and school libraries with books that reflect the experiences and interests of students.
- Invite parents and students to act as researchers, documenting the various literacy practices in their families.
- Invite students to research the past literacy and schooling experiences of family members.
- Open up spaces for children to express multiple spiritualities and literate practices.
- Recognize that the literacy practices, spiritualities, and parenting practices of families are never homogeneous.

Whether or not parents and schools can forge partnerships may very well be a function of how fluid schools and their communities become. Parents can and are willing to change, as the authors in this volume demonstrate. They become more involved in their children's education. They become leaders in their communities. But schools also must change, especially their tendency to isolate both teachers and students from the wealth of knowledge in local communities. And this will mean listening to parents' stories, understanding who they and their children are, and expanding a curriculum that bridges the school and community. But parents and teachers need spaces where they can talk about the purpose of education and the value of different curricula for helping children flourish.

In the end, we recognize that differences in communities, local contexts, and schools can be confusing to educators and researchers as we attempt to support families and children with schooling and literacy learning. In this volume, we have documented the work of educators and researchers who have found ways to build on the cultural, racial, and economic diversity of their schools and classrooms. We argue that is imperative that we extend our existing understandings of parent involvement, family literacy, and the complex relationships that exist among race, class, access, positionality, and power as we continue to work on behalf of children and families.

REFERENCES

Gruenewald, D. (2005). Foundations of place: A multidisciplinary framework for place-conscious education. *American Educational Research Journal, 40,* 619–654.

Harvey, D. (2006). *Justice, nature, & the geography of difference.* Malden, MA: Blackwell.

Harvey, D. (2007). *A brief history of neoliberalism.* New York: Oxford University Press.

hooks, b. (1990). *Yearning: Race, gender, and cultural politics.* Boston: South End Press.

Lipman, P. (2007). Education and the spatialization of urban inequality: A case study of Chicago's Renaissance 2010. In K. Gulson & C. Symes (Eds.), *Spatial theories of education: Policy and geography matters* (pp. 155–174). New York: Routledge.

AFTERWORD

The genre of "afterword," recently popular in the publishing world, reflects our continuous urge to look beyond where we have been to where we may be headed. Certain points in history, such as those marked by devastating epidemic, natural disaster, political upheaval, or financial chaos, escalate our sense of the critical need for accurate forecasting or, short of this ideal, thoughtful foreshadowing.

This afterword reaches for the latter, reflecting on what the volume *says* about where we are, and, in doing so, provoking us to think of what the volume does *not* say. What are the challenges and where are the partners not mentioned here? As this afterword does its job of foreshadowing, it points out challenges likely to continue and partners likely to grow in strength and influence in support of both parents and children in relation to formal schooling. Finally, this afterword encourages educators to use their powers of empathy and imagination as they look ahead. Too often the sheer drudgery of classroom life strips from teachers and administrators two of their greatest gifts as humans: the power to envision the possible and to create circles of empathetic actors to make the possible probable.

WHERE ARE WE NOW?

Four core themes run through the chapters of the volume: the need for a revisionist history of parent involvement; the agentive role of parents in shaping their children's learning; engagement with multimodalities in children's everyday lives; and the inevitable individualism in parents' approaches to home–school expectations. Some chapters address these themes through ideas familiar to literacy researchers and educators: "literacy practices," "local literacies," "identity," and "power relations." Reflection on these ideas leads readers to interpret these chapters in a comparative frame, along with longitudinal ethnographic studies of children and families at home (Heath, 1983/1996, 1990; Lareau, 2003; Lofty, 1992; Zentella, 1997).

The fundamental ideological orientation of the volume's authors is to set right the prevailing parents-as-problem orientation sometimes put forward by school administrators, teachers, and policymakers. Chapters illustrate the ways in which parents manage their children's opportunities to link what happens at home with classroom life and learning. As social actors, parents play primary roles as managers of their household schedules, finances, work and leisure, religious lives, and familial relationships and health. They are also performers within the labor force and in many roles other than those directly related to parenting: church deacon, caregiver for elderly parents, Scout director, volunteer at the local museum, and occasional grocery shopper and house cleaner for a younger sister sick with the flu. As a consequence of the many roles and performance spaces in which parents have to act, they neither can nor want to see their own children primarily in the role of *students*.

Children, as well as their parents, play many roles in their young lives. They are siblings, grandchildren, and nieces and nephews; sports team members; style-conscious consumers; high-demand spokespersons for scheduling of family time; instigators of friendships among families; and partners in leisure time pursuits of family members. Although schools see children primarily in the single role of student and therefore expected to adhere to the norms and values of the institution of schooling, parents see their children in a wide range of roles, with student as only one of many. The role of student, in its current interpretation by schools, includes no hint of older meanings of the term that brought with them responsibilities for discovery, exploration, and invention by students of mathematics, literature, botany, and so on. Currently, the term not only encases a passive being within a dyadic student–teacher relationship, but also ignores or belittles creative manipulation of ideas and skills beyond the domain and authority of experts credentialed by formal education institutions.

Authors of this volume see the expanding gap between these exclusionary effects of schools' policies and practices and democratic goals of education. Documented here are various ways in which the ideology, schedule, homework demands, and print-focus of schools do not take into account many parental concerns and values surrounding their children's performance in school. Several chapters illustrate how social and economic histories of family relationships, as well as parental talents and interests, shape the lives of children and parents. For example, when parents have an intense leisure-time orientation to subjects and skills (e.g., science, mathematics, literary reading), that schools value, their children have innumerable incentives to learn in similar directions. On the other hand, when parental (or older siblings') interests and orientations (e.g., sports, fishing, playing pool, videogaming, or shopping) do not readily align with school tasks and subjects, schools urge replacement of time spent in these pursuits with activities directly related to academic achievement. Yet neither parents nor children readily give up their shared loves, opportunities for joint outings, and competitive bouts of play. Many parents see having a good time with their children as primary to the mental health, respect, and development of a sense of joy in life that the young to carry into adulthood.

For these and other reasons, parents and children do not think consistently about whether leisure-time activities will (or could) translate to school subjects or contribute to concepts being practiced in homework assignments. Some areas of children's expertise (e.g., creation of comic strips or graphic novels and fan 'zines, or intense engagement with building with Lego sets) that seem "logical" in relation to school-valued skills rarely enter subject matter learning in classrooms. Teachers point out that assessment pressures and lesson-plan monitoring direct their attention almost exclusively to their students as academic learners who can master standardized grade-level curricula and assessments only by dedication to school norms and tasks. Hence neither children's hobbies and leisure-time pursuits nor parental work schedules and transportation needs are ever likely to find purpose and consideration in the life of the school.

WHAT ARE THE CHALLENGES?

Although it is certainly the case that many, if not most, parents spend enjoyable, productive, and mutually beneficial time with their children, the challenge lies in those who do not. The foster care systems of counties and cities across the United States make this point clear, as do the many reported cases of child abuse and neglect by family members. These facts make it difficult for administrators and teachers, particularly those working in highly underresourced communities, to believe and act with faith in the good intentions and actions of all parents. Across the income spectrum, many parents respect neither their own children nor their children's teachers. The intrusiveness of these parents, as well as their neglect of children's feelings and needs, pains teachers and administrators and often puts them at legal risk. Teen parents, many of whom were not parented well in terms of finding pleasure in school achievement and setting life goals, offer special challenges to teachers of young children. Family dissolution, whether through divorce, abandonment, imprisonment, or need to escape detection by immigration authorities, means that in communities across the United States, many children and adolescents reside not in a single household, but on the streets or with friends. These young people find it extremely difficult to think of themselves as *students* when they are playing roles that many adults find overwhelming. These and other circumstances that place the health and welfare of U.S. children near the bottom in rankings of economically advanced nations, show little signs of diminishing in the near future.

As states across the country decrease their education budgets and class sizes increase, while at the same time counseling and social service supports decrease, even the most well-intentioned teachers and administrators cannot keep pace with the needs of their students and parents. Kindergarten and early elementary teachers who learn of home conditions that threaten the health and safety as well as the academic promise of their young learners, have neither the time nor the means to follow up with resources. Thus only the most severe and obvious cases of neglect or abuse get passed on to the social service bureaucracy. Their case loads, and the difficulty of tracking the whereabouts of family members or responsible guardians, make rapid and successful intervention more unlikely than anyone would wish. Teachers, especially those at the middle- and secondary-school levels, have few ways of learning even the barest details of their students' lives and less chance of doing anything significant to ameliorate their situations. Moreover, even for young children, interference from school authorities that could suggest parental neglect or abuse, carries legal risks and sometimes personal threats from parents who feel wronged. Tracking too carefully the "real" parents of immigrant children can lead to deportation of one or more parents and therefore result in family dissolution. In essence, parent–child relations will never be transparent, congruent, or easy for even the most well-meaning and diligent among school authorities and teachers. Hence, caution is called for in setting out broad policies and practices based on generalizations about parent involvement in schools.

WHERE ARE PARTNERS?

In many instances, children themselves have found partners that can help them meet challenges addressed by neither schools nor families. In some cases, social workers and probation officers have located support beyond school and parent for young members of families in crisis. These partners range from grassroots community organizations to nationally affiliated youth groups (such as Scouts or Boys and Girls Clubs) and from religious groups to sports teams. In these settings, the young find peer support, activities in which they can test their talents, and adults whose job does not depend on assessing the extent to which the young excel in responding to subject matter instruction. Whether sports teams, arts centers, environmental projects, or community service groups, these learning environments enable the young to play numerous roles. Children and adolescents work and play within a safe and predictable system of rules and have multiple channels and opportunities to advance their responsibilities. Most of these partners give young people different types of platforms on which to show what they can do, model, create, imagine, practice, plan, and manage in collaboration with peers.

As yet, ideologies surrounding public education do not acknowledge the full learning life that the young have beyond school and family. Thus, with very few exceptions, public school systems have no sustainable bridges across which children's talents beyond subject matter achievement can be recognized and used. Children live not only within families, but also in communities that include playgrounds, sports fields, libraries, youth organizations, religious groups, medical facilities, and public servants who have a wide array of interactions and dimensions of influence with the young. Although venerated educators such as John Dewey, James Coleman, and Edward Gordon have set out both the philosophy and practical means to build a comprehensive approach to learning that embraces families, communities, and schools, only sporadic experiments have attempted to create the infrastructure needed to do so.

Where schools are concerned, a curious disconnect exists between espoused philosophy of democratic ideals and fearsome realities. Whereas the post-Civil Rights decades of the 1970s and 1980s led us to valorize the dignity and promise of taking everyday life and "cultural" ways into classrooms, the dangers of this easy dichotomy became quickly evident to many. The "post" critics of structuralism, colonialism, and modernism railed against such simplistic dichotomies, while field-based anthropologists and migration sociologists pointed repeatedly to the permeability of ethnic, racial, and even class identities under different situational realities. Philosophers, empiricists, and theoreticians urged academics and policymakers to take care in generalizing about the "sources of the self" (Taylor, 1989). All cautioned that rapidly increasing global expansion of niche interests and of technologies linking individuals and groups with shared interests together would dislodge long-standing estimations of standard credentialing for authoritative knowledge and skills. This reality means that voluntary expertise development—by young and old learning outside both families and formal education—is likely to expand with increasing speed as a societal phenomenon in information-based economies.

Young people in these societies become at younger and younger ages masters of accessing information and entertainment via the Internet and of understanding how to manipulate software and hardware. In doing so, they rapidly organize, orchestrate, and manage their own time and thereby find ways to advance skills and information they perceive themselves to need. They have modeled for their elders the pleasures and achievements that result from voluntarily seeking areas of expertise. Now young and old increasingly recognize and assert that they must decide what and how they want to learn, unfettered by certified authorities or formal education requirements, schedules, and age-grading or age limitations (cf. Lewis and Norton, this volume).

Few would deny that the bulk of learning associated with information and communication technologies now takes place informally among those with special interests. Teenagers teach their parents and grandparents how to use their cell phones and urge them to search the Web and to stay alert to the new possibilities Web 2.0 offers. Hospitals and medical doctors expect their patients to use the Internet not only to seek information but to confirm appointments, receive reports from medical tests, and refill prescriptions. Increasingly, businesses create work environments to facilitate the unfettered transfer of creative transformation that comes through watching others and undertaking experimentation.

Business environments have given us the term *long tail learning* to characterize what will happen as advanced economies increasingly shift away from a focus on a relatively small number of products and markets at the *head* of the popularity curve toward a huge number of niches in the *tail* (Anderson, 2006). This change means a shift from a *consumer culture* (largely passive in the consumption of finished goods) to a *participation culture* in which people have the associates (e.g., friends, family members, or experts willing to advise), motivation, and means of access that enable them to participate actively in personally meaningful problems and learning needs they themselves define. Already Web 2.0 demonstrates the shift away from an *authoritative* model of *given* information filtered by experts toward a *distributed* model of created, assessed, designed, multimedia information that provides for wider and richer *ecologies of participation and learning.*

In essence, education theorists, such as anthropologist Jean Lave, psychologist Barbara Rogoff, and others, have expressed the same idea for more than 2 decades. Yet neither primary and secondary schools nor higher education institutions have rearranged their structures, expectations, and assessments to line up with what increasingly is becoming unmistakable as the future of learning in complex economies around the globe. In this future, parents will play a role in helping to be models of long tail learning in their array of interests and means of "keeping up" with what is happening around the world in relation to these interests. Parents, as well as community members in organizations such as sports groups, libraries, theatres, and gyms, can provide apprenticeship opportunities and technological access to information. But neither parents nor schools will be likely to play central roles in learning for the "long tail." Blocking schools' recognition of long tail learning is the inability of institutions of formal education to see relations between act and consequence. Unable to do so, they will remain unable to plan, create, and implement alternative future narratives for themselves in concert with the increasing speed of technological changes and employer needs. *Reform* of schools is the drumbeat. Dictated by technological forces and rapidly shifting socialization conditions for the young are creative collaborations among learning environments that include every possible resource from museums and parks to highly specialized cross-age campuses of research and development that bring art, business, environmental sustainability, science, and ethics together. Keeping this kind of change from happening is the fact that schools are places of employment that depend on replication of themselves and the continuation of operational norms grounded on power and authority, standardization and control. To alter these norms would put at risk jobs, job training, and systems of regulation long established in education.

Yet the human capacity to see through power, work around and with it, and make opportunities to learn in spite of contrarian authoritative dictates has been attested to for centuries. To underspecify and refuse to recognize these competencies and the extraordinary human talent for acting on curiosity is to place societies at risk. In the lives of individuals in contemporary economically advanced societies, what matters most in learning is motivated, practiced, perfected, and adapted or abandoned beyond the formal institutions of family and schools. Thus the most promising partners likely to join together to keep on creating learning environments not yet dreamed of even in the wildest of our imaginations, are the young themselves. Platitude though it has become, shaping the future lies in their hands, minds, and will.

—*Shirley Brice Heath*
Brown University
Stanford University

REFERENCES

Anderson, C. (2006). *The long tail: Why the future of business is selling less of more.* New York: Hyperion.

Heath, S. B. (1996). *Ways with words: Language, life, and work in communities and classrooms*. Cambridge: Cambridge University Press. (Original work published 1983)

Heath, S. B. (1990). The children of Trackton's children: Spoken and written language in social change. In J. W. Stigler, R. A. Shweder, & G. S. Herdt (Eds.), *Cultural psychology: The Chicago symposia on human development* (pp. 496–519). New York: Cambridge University Press.

Lareau, A. (2003). *Unequal childhoods: Class, race, and family life*. Berkeley: University of California Press.

Lofty, J. S. (1992). *Time to write: The influence of time and culture on learning to write*. Albany: State University of New York Press.

Taylor, C. (1989). *Sources of the self*. Cambridge, MA: Harvard University Press.

Zentella, A. (1997). *Growing up bilingual*. London: Blackwell.

ABOUT THE CONTRIBUTORS

Catherine Compton-Lilly is an assistant professor in curriculum and instruction at the University of Wisconsin–Madison and previously taught in the public schools for 18 years. Dr. Compton-Lilly has written several books and authored articles in the *Reading Research Quarterly, Research in the Teaching of English, The Reading Teacher, The Journal of Early Childhood Literacy, Literacy Teaching and Learning,* and *Language Arts.* Her interests include examining how time operates as a contextual factor in children's lives as they progress through school and construct their identities as students and readers.

Susana Y. Flores is an educator in the School Readiness Program at the El Rancho Unified School District in Pico Rivera, CA. She has worked in the field of education for over 20 years. Her experience as an immigrant and English Language Learner has informed her research and practice. She has worked as a teacher assistant in outdoor education, a science teacher, an ESL middle school teacher, a research program evaluator, a university professor in bilingual bicultural studies, and professional development. Dr. Flores co-founded the *Journal of Latinos and Education,* authored articles in various educational journals, and co-edited the book *Post Critical Ethnography.* Her interests include Linguistic and Cultural Minorities in the United States. She is also a mother of two bilingual children and very involved in their school's local school site council, ELAC and PTA.

Stuart Greene is an associate professor of English and director of the undergraduate minor in an education program, "Education, Schooling, and Society." He has also served as the O'Malley Director of the University Writing Program and Associate Dean for Undergraduate Studies in Arts and Letters at Notre Dame. His research focuses on the history of education, civil rights legislation, and minority opportunity in public schools. This work has led to the publication of his co-edited volume, *Making Race Visible: Literacy Research for Racial Understanding,* for which he won the National Council of Teachers of English Richard A. Meade Award in 2005.

He also edited *Literacy as a Civil Right* and co-directs a parent involvement project, No Parent Left Behind, in the South Bend community.

Tisha Y. Lewis is an assistant professor in reading education at Georgia State University. She is a past recipient of the J. Michael Parker Award from the National Reading Conference and of the NCTE Research Foundation's Cultivating New Voices Among Scholars of Color Fellowship Program. Dr. Lewis's interests explore how agency, identity, and power among African American families are constructed as they use digital literacies as mediating tools to make sense of their lives.

Joyce F. Long is an educational consultant and adjunct faculty member at the University of Notre Dame. She teaches courses on educational psychology, creativity, and community-based research in the Education, Schooling, and Society Minor. She also co-directs No Parent Left Behind, a parent involvement program. Her articles and book chapters relate to teaching, learning, and motivation.

Nadjwa E.L. Norton is an associate professor in the Transformative Literacy Program at City College, CUNY. She has taught from preschool to high school in both public and private schools in urban areas. Dr. Norton's research agenda focuses on spiritualities, children's hip-hop literacies practices, critical literacies of children, and children/youth co-researcher methodologies. Her work has appeared in *Language Arts, Journal of Literacy and Technology, Education and Urban Society, Disability Studies Quarterly, Urban Review,* and *The Feminist Teacher.*

Darren O'Brien is the parent of two children in the St. Louis Public Schools. Darren serves as the vice president of the Parent Teacher Organization at his children's school and has been on its board for 3 years. He has worked on the issues of lead in the Public School buildings, as well as the effort to maintain local control of the school district. Darren works at the Genome Sequencing Center at the Washington University Medical school. Darren is also a musician and when not working or playing music with friends, is camping, hiking, or traveling somewhere in the world.

Rosario Ordoñez-Jasis is an associate professor in the reading department at California State University, Fullerton, and has worked with teachers, students, and their families in urban public schools for over 15 years. Dr. Ordoñez-Jasis has authored articles in *the Journal of Early Childhood Teacher Education, Reading Teacher, Journal of Latinos in Education, Young Children,*

The High School Journal, Urban Review, and *the Journal of Social Justice.* Her research investigates the impact of language, culture, and identity in the literacy lives of Latino children. Dr. Ordoñez-Jasis has two small boys and is currently working on a First Five California literacy initiative in Los Angeles, California.

Rebecca Rogers is an associate professor in the College of Education at the University of Missouri–St. Louis. Her research focuses on the sociopolitical contexts of literacy and language education both in and out of schools. She is the author of several books, including her latest, *Designing Socially Just Learning Communities: Critical Literacy Across the Lifespan* (with Melissa Mosley and Mary Ann Kramer). Her research has been published in journals such as *Reading Research Quarterly, Linguistics and Education, Language Arts, Journal of Literacy Research, Race, Ethnicity and Education* and *Teacher Education.* She is the co-founder of a grassroots teacher group called the Literacy for Social Justice Group. In 2009 Rogers was a Fulbright Fellow at the Unversidad Nacional de San Martín in Buenos Aires, Argentina. She currently serves as an elected board member for the St. Louis Public School district.

Caitlin L. Ryan is an assistant professor of curriculum and instruction in the College of Education at East Carolina University. She previously worked for a community-based organization called Heads Up, teaching literacy enrichment programs in the Washington, DC public schools. Dr. Ryan's work has been published in *Language Arts* and *Linguistics in Education.* Her research interests revolve around the relationships among literacy, children's literature, social positioning, and educational equity for children in elementary schools.

Patricia Snell is a doctoral candidate in the Department of Sociology at the University of Notre Dame. She received her B.A. in Sociology and Psychology from the University of Arizona in 2000, her M.S.W. in community practice from the University of Denver in 2006, and her M.A. in Sociology from the University of Notre Dame in 2008. Snell's publications include articles published with *Journal of Adolescent Research,* and *Educational Action Research* and coauthor of two books, *Souls in Transition: The Religious and Spiritual Lives of Emerging Adults* and *Passing the Plate: Why American Christians Don't Give Away More Money.* Her interests involve investigating the ways people and communities respond to socioeconomic inequalities in organizational social settings such as schools, religious congregations, and nonprofits.

INDEX